Cricketing Allsorts

The Good, The Bad, The Ugly (and The Downright Weird)

EDITED BY JO HARMAN

FOREWORD BY DAVID "BUMBLE" LLOYD

BLOOMSBURY

LONDON • OXFORD • NEW YORK • NEW DELHI • SYDNEY

John Wisden & Co Ltd
An imprint of Bloomsbury Publishing Plc

50 Bedford Square   1385 Broadway
London   New York
WC1B 3DP   NY10018
UK   USA

www.bloomsbury.com

WISDEN and the wood-engraving device are trademarks of John Wisden & Company
Ltd, a subsidiary of Bloomsbury Publishing Plc

First published 2017
© All Out Cricket 2017

www.wisden.com
www.wisdenrecords.com
Follow Wisden on Twitter @WisdenAlmanack
and on Facebook at Wisden Sports

British Library Cataloguing-in-Publication Data
A catalogue record for this book is available from the British Library.

Library of Congress Cataloguing-in-Publication data has been applied for.

ISBN: HB: 978-1-4729-4344-6
ePub: 978-1-4729-4345-3

2 4 6 8 10 9 7 5 3 1

Typeset in Sentinel 9.5pt by All Out Cricket
Printed and bound in China by C&C Offset Printing Co

Bloomsbury Publishing Plc makes every effort to ensure that the papers used in the
manufacture of our books are natural, recyclable products made from wood grown in
well-managed forests. Our manufacturing processes conform to the environmental
regulations of the country of origin.

To find out more about our authors and books visit www.wisden.com. Here you will
find extracts, author interviews, details of forthcoming events and the option to sign
up for our newsletters.

"I TEND TO THINK THAT CRICKET IS THE
GREATEST THING THAT GOD CREATED ON EARTH."
HAROLD PINTER

"I WANT TO PLAY CRICKET; IT DOESN'T SEEM TO
MATTER IF YOU WIN OR LOSE."
MEATLOAF

"WHAT A WONDERFUL CURE FOR INSOMNIA."
GROUCHO MARX

Contents

FOREWORD   **vii**

The Good

EPIC COUNTY CHAMPIONSHIP SEASONS   **3**
LEAVES AND LEAVERS   **9**
BUMBLE'S GREATEST UMPIRES   **13**
ASHES CATCHES   **19**
LONE RANGERS   **25**
FORGOTTEN GEMS   **31**
MEMORABLE SIXES   **37**
ENGLAND'S GREATEST UNCAPPED PLAYERS   **41**
DYNASTIES   **47**
IRRESISTIBLE COMEBACKS   **57**
BOWLING PARTNERSHIPS   **63**
CRICKETING LOVE AFFAIRS   **69**
SOLDIERS   **75**

The Bad

VILLAGE MOMENTS   **81**
UNFORTUNATE ENGLAND CAREERS   **87**
NOTORIOUS DROPS   **93**
ACCURSED GONGS   **99**
WORST OVERS   **105**
NIGHTMARE SEASONS   **109**
BUNNIES   **115**
THE NEW BOTHAMS   **119**
UGLY DUCKS   **125**
RUN OUT NINETY-NINES   **131**

The Ugly

INFAMOUS INTERVIEWS 137
TV VEHICLES 143
CRICKILEAKS 149
INDECENT EXPOSURES 155
HYSTERICAL OVERREACTIONS 159
FIGHTS AND FEUDS 167
BRAZEN PRODUCT ENDORSEMENTS 173
HEAVY GRUBBERS 177
LEGAL BATTLES 183
SEND-OFFS 189

The Downright Weird

UNLIKELIEST FANS 195
FICTIONAL CHARACTERS 201
ICONIC FASHION STATEMENTS 207
IMPERSONATIONS 211
BORROWED KIT 217
HOAXES AND IMPOSTERS 223
JOBS FOR THE BOYS (AND GIRLS) 229
CHEESE! 235
NICKNAMES 239
UNUSUAL CAPTAINS 245
TRIBUTES TO CRICKET 249
REMARKABLE JOURNEYS 255
UNLIKELY STATISTICAL QUIRKS 259
GAMES WITHIN A GAME 265
CRICKET SONGS 269

ACKNOWLEDGEMENTS 275

INDEX 276

Foreword

BY DAVID "BUMBLE" LLOYD

For 50 years I've been involved in this game, as a player, coach, commentator and fan, and it still gets me going even now. Cricket has a reputation for being a bit stuck in its ways – for sure there's something in that, but you name me a sport that's changed more dramatically over the past decade. I've followed it all my life and I'm still learning new things.

For me, cricket is about enjoying yourself and playing with a smile on your face. Sure, it's a serious business these days – with all this money swirling around, big contracts, flash tournaments – but it's hardly life and death. Relax. Enjoy it. It's only cricket!

I've always thought it's best when played hard but fair, with some room for humour along the way. We saw it in the excellent 2016 Test series between England and Pakistan. Neither team gave an inch but the contest was played in the right spirit, with Misbah-ul-Haq, well into his forties, doing those press-ups at Lord's after he got his hundred. Brilliant. England's players might not have liked it but it was great theatre and the fans loved it, and that's what it's all about. Or the time back in 1996, when I was coach of England, and I told our No.11 Alan Mullally – who was a hopeless batsman – that I'd buy him 30 pints of Guinness if he made it to 30 against Wasim and Waqar. Big Al didn't quite manage it, but he did make his best Test score of 24!

It's these quirks and eccentricities that stick in the mind and make cricket special. From the outside looking in they might seem difficult to grasp, but once cricket gets its claws in you, it doesn't let go easily. This book has loads of great examples of that quirkiness, and loads of great stories involving characters I've played with and against or commentated on.

I've even chipped in myself, picking out my choice of the ten greatest umpires of all time. It's never been an easy gig being an umpire – I should know, I tried it myself for several years – and the introduction of DRS, while in theory there to help the umpires, has also made life a bit more complicated for them in some ways. Mistakes are highlighted in a way they never were when I was standing in the middle. It is nice to be able to pay tribute to the best I've seen who did a difficult job very well indeed.

The great characters, outstanding performances and entertaining mishaps featured in this book help to sum up why I fell for the game and why, so many years later, I'm still completely hooked. So sit back, put your feet up and enjoy the best, worst, ugliest and weirdest that cricket has to offer. ∎

The
Good

No game has such a high opinion of itself – wrapped, of course, in all those layers of angst – as the grand old knockabout they call cricket. Turfs are hallowed, whites are pristine, pavilions grand and bowlers electrifying. There's a whole vocabulary out there, designed to assert itself not just over every other "sport" – as if cricket should ever be compared to such things! – but pretty much every other pursuit known to humankind. Witness then, over the following pages, stories of great dynasties and irresistible comebacks rubbing up perfectly well next to the best leaves, hardiest soldiers and fieriest love affairs known to cricketing humanity. Read of brutish spells and inspiring mentors, of fabulous inventions and titanic ties. Luxuriate in the greatest World Cup cameos and the finest last-wicket stands. Cricket spends almost as much time patting itself on the back as it does tearing its hair out... it really is a very troubled genius.

Epic County Championship Seasons

WHEN THAT PATCH STAYS PURPLE FOR A WHOLE SUMMER...

10) TONY FROST, 2008

1,003 runs at 83.58, two centuries

Warwickshire's bespectacled keeper had laid down the gloves in 2006 to pursue a career as a groundsman, bringing a decade of diligent but unspectacular service to a close. However, he was unexpectedly cajoled out of retirement when England called up Tim Ambrose. Frost scored 46 not out in his first match for two years, 90 in his next and boatloads thereafter, finishing the campaign with a career-best 242 not out. Having planned to spend his season on a lawnmower, Frosty the yeoman finished it on top of the Championship batting averages.

9) DENIS COMPTON AND BILL EDRICH, 1947

Compton: 2,003 runs at 96.80, 11 centuries; Edrich: 2,257 runs at 77.82, eight centuries

---

"They go together in English cricket as Gilbert and Sullivan go together in English opera," wrote RC Robertson-Glasgow, and in 1947 the Middlesex pair belted out classic after classic to rewrite the record books. In all first-class cricket they scored 7,335 runs, took 140 wickets and held 66 catches between them. Middlesex won their first title for 26 years and John Robertson – 2,214 runs at 65.11 – was left to wonder how he'd finished third in the county's batting averages.

8) MUSHTAQ AHMED, 2003
103 wickets at 24.65, ten five-wicket hauls, five ten-wicket hauls

Sussex hadn't won a County Championship until the Pakistani leggie's arrival. In the six seasons he spent at Hove, they won it three times. The duck was broken in 2003 when Mushy became the first bowler since Courtney Walsh in 1998 to take 100-plus wickets in a Championship campaign. He repeated the trick in 2006 – no bowler has hit the 100-wicket landmark since – and took 90 the following season as the south-coasters won back-to-back titles.

7) DAVID FULTON, 2001
1,729 runs at 78.59, eight centuries

After nine seasons of mediocrity in which he'd mustered seven centuries – with his greatest claim to fame facing Wasim in a floppy hat in the 1995 B&H final – Kent's skipper found himself on the verge of an England call-up after a gluttonous campaign that featured nine tons (eight of them in the Championship). Nasser Hussain later revealed that England's selectors had chosen Fulton for the Headingley Ashes Test in place of Mark Butcher after the Surrey man had broken curfew, only to have a late change of heart. As it was, Butch batted rather nicely for his 173 not out and Fulton returned to the shires.

6) MICKY STEWART, 1957
1,290 at 33.94, two centuries; 63 catches

Stewart's run haul was healthy enough in Surrey's title-winning campaign but it's his superlative fielding at short-leg that sees him make this list. Under ultra-aggressive captain Stuart Surridge, Surrey took the innovative step of crowding batsmen with close fielders, allowing them to take catches off defensive shots if they dared stand close enough. Surridge had retired by 1957 but the philosophy was ingrained and Stewart was the ideal man to station at boot hill. Fearless and agile, he took 77 catches in all first-class cricket including a world-record seven in an innings at Northampton.

5) PHIL SIMMONS, 1996

1,186 runs at 56.47, four centuries; 56 wickets at 18.23, three five-wicket hauls

West Indian Simmons' modest record didn't scream "marquee signing" when he arrived at Leicestershire. However, in a roster of overseas players that included Walsh, Ambrose, Pollock and Bevan, come September there was no doubting the star turn. A beefed up Simmons was in full beast-mode, bowling faster than ever, whacking it miles and catching pigeons at slip. The Trinidadian inspired an unfancied side to their first Championship title in 21 years and became the first player to take over 50 wickets and score more than 1,000 runs in a Championship season since Kevin Curran in 1990. Will Gidman is the only man to achieve the feat since.

4) GRAEME HICK, 1988

2,443 runs at 76.34, nine centuries

England were counting down the days until Harare-born Hick qualified to represent them. It became almost too tantalising to bear when in 1988 – still three years before he became eligible – the 21-year-old became only the second batsman since World War II to score 1,000 first-class runs before the end of May, helped along by a mammoth 405 not out at Taunton. Hick topped the Championship run-scoring charts for the third year in succession and led Worcestershire to their first title since 1974.

3) PHIL MEAD, 1928

2,843 runs at 81.22, 12 centuries

A batting colossus for Hampshire for over 30 years, Mead scored more Championship runs than any man before or since – just the

46,268 of them – and topped 2,000 in a campaign on nine occasions. "He was never much concerned with breaking records," said John Arlott. Pity really, because he was very good at it. The left-hander's tour de force came in 1928 when, at the age of 41, he racked up 3,000 first-class runs including a record 2,843 in the Championship.

2) MARK RAMPRAKASH, 2006
2.211 runs at 105.28, eight centuries

Ramps had been in imperious form since arriving at Surrey in 2001 but this was the season when he really took it up a notch. He made a career-best 292 against Gloucestershire, topped that with a triple against Northants and passed 2,000 runs in his 20th innings – a new record. His campaign included a string of 150-plus scores in five consecutive matches – another new record – but wasn't enough to get him in the Ashes tour party. It seemed like a one-off, a feat never to be repeated, but then he went and did it again in 2007, hitting 2,026 at 101.30.

1) TICH FREEMAN, 1933
252 wickets at 14.84, 33 five-wicket hauls, 14 ten-wicket hauls

It's testimony to the sublime skills of Alfred Percy Freeman, known to all as Tich, that in 1933 the great Hedley Verity snared 153 victims and was still the best part of a hundred wickets short of Kent's leggie. Only Wilfred Rhodes, who played nearly twice as many matches, has more than Freeman's 3,776 first-class scalps, and Freeman is one of only six men to have taken more than 200 wickets in a County Championship season, doing it on six occasions between 1928 and 1935, the last of those at the ripe old age of 47. For skill, stamina and prolificacy, Freeman has had no equal in the county game. ■

Graeme Hick
in full flow for
Worcestershire

Robin Smith had
impressive powers
of evasion

Leaves and Leavers

ONLY IN CRICKET CAN THE ACT OF DOING BASICALLY NOTHING GET TO FEEL SO DANGEROUS AND COOL

10) SMITH'S ONE-HANDER

Robin Smith. Goggle-eyed, shadow-batting through the gears, bobbing and weaving like an unbeaten middleweight, offering out the quickest they've got, and all before he's faced a ball. Everything was ramped up with the Judge. He liked getting hit, it got him going. Even his trademark leave was dramatic, involving the dominant top hand wresting the blade from the bottom hand in the heroic last-ditch act of yanking it out of the road.

9) GOWER'S FAREWELL

The leave alone. An *art*. Who and what you are. Gower's leave, as with his game, an extension of himself. There he'd stay, leg side, leftfield, those blue-stockinged feet languidly non-committal, the ball a weekend rendezvous to be ushered goodbye with a shrug on the platform. But there was poignancy, too, in Goldenhare's story; *twice* in a Test match against Pakistan he left alone a moment too late, both times disturbing his stumps from the inside edge. And in his final ever Test innings, the leave betrayed him one last time, Waqar pickpocketing his off-bail with barely a soul noticing what had happened. Even in death there was grace.

8) BELL'S TRAINSPOTTER

The Duke sees it early. Conceives the shot in his beautiful red mind. It's wide, down that corridor where he used to prod. It's there to cut, just behind point. Crouches into position. Prepares for execution. But experience speaks. Taught him much. He lets it go past, watching it go, tracing its path all the way to the keeper, a trainspotter marking a passing locomotive. Releasing himself from the pose a few seconds later, he plays that cut shot, dabbing down on thin air. I could've, he says. If I'd wanted to. Next time, next time.

7) CLOSE'S CHEST PASS

More of a "go to" than a "leave alone", but then that was Brian Close: balding, forty-something and helmetless, recalled to face the Babylonian fire of Holding and Roberts in '76, and wearing them time after time flush on the chest. The only surprise was that he didn't trap it and volley it on the bounce straight back from whence it came.

6) PONTING'S LUNGE

Throughout the last decade, nothing said "580-4 declared" quite like the Punter mega-lunge on a crisp Australian morning. England will have just nipped out one of the lefties (they can't both smash it every time) to be met by No.3 sashaying across the turf. Get him early, lads; *get him early*. The first ball is a pearler: up there, seaming, rising steeply. *Early*. And he's seen it, and the front foot's advancing, and it keeps on coming, hamstrings in peril, and he's low, weight bent over front knee (on guard!) and the arms are up in supplication, and the hands are clasped high above the head, a world champion in laurels, and the ball's an irrelevance now, a piffling pie, and though he's not yet played a shot, you know, you just *know*, how many there are to come.

5) TRESCO'S LINEMAN

The leave as respectful nod to gentlemanly manners. Unshowy, technically clever and totally in keeping with the man. Not so much a leave as a deliberate play and miss, Trescothick, a leftie, figured that by playing inside the line of the angled delivery and refusing to follow it, he eliminated the chances of being bowled or nicking off, all the while dangling the false hope of a moral victory to the gently steaming bowler. Canny.

4) KP'S WINDSCREEN WIPER

Everything with Kev is done for effect. He has two leaves, both very much him. For the first example, refer back to Ponting's power-drunk lunge; for the second, imagine a man using his bat to imitate a windscreen wiper by pulling his evading hands *across* his body. It's broadly unnecessary but noteworthy nonetheless; and that's Pietersen for you. It implies to the bowler and his adoring millions that he's undertaken full analysis of every minuscule variance of the delivery in question – considering its potency, weighing his chances, pondering the morsel – before finally, cutely, pulling out with absolute conviction. It could be saying: well bowled! It's actually saying: I'll have you.

3) READ'S MISREAD

Plenty have done it. It's not uncommon to misread the slower ball and get duped into thinking it's a beamer when in fact it's a floaty bomb destined for the bootlaces. But few could ever have looked so startled, so bewildered, so utterly lost, as Chris Read did in just his second Test innings. It was 1999. England were the wrong side of ordinary. Chris Cairns was in his pomp. The boy was on nought at Lord's when a looping bundle of deceit dropped out of the air and through Read's legs as he cowered for cover. The outstretched arms that followed and incredulous look on his face were almost too sad for words. Not that there was much sympathy going round at the time. Only when Graham Thorpe did the same thing against a Courtney Walsh slowie a year later did Read get to breathe again.

2) COURTNEY'S BUSINESSMAN

Talking of which, the Richard Pryor of tailenders was without doubt the funniest batsman to ever play the game. With exaggerated swagger in direct inversion of his own crapness, here was a strutting octopus of a No.11, all bulging eyes, alien-hand syndrome and inexplicable legs, topped off with a hammy leave-alone that somehow evoked an adulterous businessman briskly walking down the garden path, head in the air, folding his newspaper-bat primly under his arm as he goes. Nothing to see here, old boy! Now get back to your mark.

1) CLARKE'S POSE

Every Englishman's favourite leave belongs of course to Michael Clarke. Yep, it's 2005 again, and the peroxide hedgehog's epic refusal to recognise Simon Jones' banana ball. Technically, the leave was flawless: perfect transference of weight, high hands, head down, full stride out to the ball. Obligingly, Clarke held the pose for an hour or so afterwards, every ticking second accentuating the technical perfection of the non-shot. And that takes class. *Real* class. ∎

Bumble's Greatest Umpires

A FORMER FIRST-CLASS UMPIRE HIMSELF,
HERE ARE BUMBLE'S CHAMPIONS OF
THE WHITE-COATED ART

10) ROY PALMER (1942–) & KENNY PALMER (1937–)

I couldn't split them, the brothers Palmer, so they're in together. Somerset men, Kenny "Pedlar" Palmer and his sibling, the Judge – after the western character Judge Roy Bean – were both top decision-makers. Pedlar was a steely-eyed man, with a nice sense of humour, whereas Roy used to shoot you out, true to his gunslinger namesake, with the slowest raised "trigger-finger" in the west (country).

ROY: TESTS: 2 (1992–93) **ODIs:** 8 (1983–95)
KENNY: TESTS: 22 (1978–94) **ODIs:** 23 (1977–2001)

9) DAVID CONSTANT (1941–)

Always umpiring with a smile on his face, I think Connie was unlucky in the way he fell foul of officialdom and that was unfair. When he was out there and at his best he was the sort of fella that brought the fun out during a day's play – he was the life and soul of the game. And as an umpire I'd rate him as one of the very best at explaining things properly to you – why things were happening as they were and why he'd made the decision he had.

TESTS: 36 (1971–88) **ODIs:** 33 (1972–2001)

8) HARRY BALDWIN (1860–1935)

Harry used to umpire in the longest coat of all time – almost down to the floor, it was. And to count the balls in the over he used to flick coins from his left hand across to his right – it was his trademark, the way he used to do it. He had enormous ten-to-two feet and all, which made him look even funnier.

7) ALAN WHITEHEAD (1940–)

I know that Alan wasn't everyone's cup of tea as an umpire, but I can say that he was comfortably one of the very best to stand with. He had a bit of a reputation for looking for controversy on the field, and you were best advised, as a player, not to mess with him. He was also an umpire who loved his fitness training. I remember him going for a run in the Parks at Oxford once and found himself bitten by a dog! Alan's reaction to the bite was to thump the owner! Having said all of that, there was no one more loyal to stand with. And no one that would back you on the field quite like Alan did.
TESTS: 5 (1982–87) **ODIs:** 14 (1979–2001)

6) SIMON TAUFEL (1971–)

Alongside Aleem Dar, I would put Simon Taufel right up there with the very best technical umpires. He became an international umpire at a young age but immediately commanded respect, despite not having a professional playing career himself, and won the ICC Umpire of the Year award on many occasions.
TESTS: 74 (2000–2012) **ODIs:** 174 (1999–2012)

5) BILL ALLEY (1919–2004)

Bill was so funny. One of the funniest blokes you could ever wish to be on the field with – a great sense of humour. I remember him catching Lancashire's Peter Lee picking the seam one day. And

Bill had a fair reputation for doing the same, during his playing days. He shouted across to Peter, tossing him the ball after examining it, saying: "You've done a brilliant job with that – so good in fact that if you don't get seven-fer, I'll report you!"
TESTS: 10 (1974–81) **ODIs:** 9 (1974–81)

4) SYD BULLER (1909–70)

Syd was the first of what you might call the celebrity umpires. It was deemed an honour to play in a game that was being officiated over by him. He was a disciplinarian and a figure of great authority and also of huge standing in the game.
TESTS: 33 (1956–69)

3) BILLY BOWDEN (1963–)

Billy is an old-fashioned character – a real personality and someone I call a friend. I think his decision-making is exemplary and I also love the way he umpires with a smile on his face and a twinkle in his eye.
TESTS: 84 (2000–) **ODIs:** 200 (1995–)

2) ARTHUR JEPSON (1915–97)

There must be a million stories about Jepo. He had this head of slicked-back hair – it definitely wasn't Brylcreem holding it in place – it was more likely chip fat! He was indiscreet, insensitive and unbelievably funny on the field. He had a big booming voice, which used to echo around the stands. I remember him commenting on Neal Radford's bowling. Radders was struggling for a bit of rhythm on the day. "'Ere, can he bat?" shouted Arthur from his position at square leg. And before anyone could confirm or deny the question, he said, "'Cos he can't f***ing bowl. And he runs up like he's crapped himself!"
TESTS: 4 (1966–69) **ODIs:** 5 (1974–76)

1) RAY JULIAN (1936–)

I don't think there's ever been an umpire that was as complete as Ray Julian. He was wonderful company to stand with, incredibly popular with the players and a far better umpire than his self-deprecating sense of humour suggested. I remember sitting back after umpiring a game together and he shouted across the room, "Well, Mr Lloyd, another perfect day for me – I'm not sure about you!"

Ray had a reputation as an umpire that "kept the game moving", shall we say. A reputation he played up to. He loved standing at Richard Hadlee's end when the tyro was playing for Nottinghamshire in the Eighties. Ray would always find out in advance which end Sir Richard was bowling. He also was unafraid to give tough decisions, never shied away from anything. For me, as well as being a prince of a bloke, Ray was spot on.

ODIs: 6 (1996–2001) ∎

Arthur Jepson: slicker than your average umpire

Andrew Strauss
took flight to dismiss
Adam Gilchrist

Ashes Catches

GLORIOUS GRABS, SENSATIONAL
SNAFFLES AND PARADISIACAL
POUCHES FROM THE ASHES ANNALS

10) WUNDERBAR MCGRATH

Fast bowlers with spindly limbs and chips on their shoulders aren't in it for the fielding. They're meant to graze, sulk, get riled, and reluctantly employ "the big size 12" when forced into action. Australians don't work like that. At Adelaide in 2002, the previously flaky Michael Vaughan was in the midst of some weird English dream where everything he struck turned to boundaries. He was on 41 in the second dig after a first-innings 177 when another effortless pick-up off the hip seemed arrowed for the rope. But the might of McGrath's outstretched dive, bucket-hands and horribly competitive spirit combined to pluck the ball millimetres from the godless Australian turf. England collapsed, and England lost.

9) PHILLIPS GIVEN THE BOOT

Wayne Phillips buried his face in his gloved hands and tried to hold back the tears. It was the dying embers of Edgbaston in 1985 and Australia were close to saving it. Phillips whacked Phil Edmonds off the back foot, the ball ricocheted off Allan Lamb's instep, and David Gower, standing insouciantly close at silly point, pocketed the ballooning ball. Gower enquired, and the umpires happily obliged, despite having next to no clue whether it had bounced. No matter, this was Gower's summer. The Ashes fell into his palms soon after.

8) DAMN FINE DILLEY

In the first Test of the 1981 series, beleaguered England skipper Ian Botham shelled two chances in the slips. Australia won by five wickets and captain Beef was honest enough to admit England would have won if they'd caught their catches. A few transformative weeks later at Leeds, Gatting was tumbling, Taylor was bouncing, and Botham himself was grabbing them off his bootstraps. Then the big one: Willis, around the wicket to the lefty Rod Marsh, the top-edged hook and a back-pedalling Graham Dilley at fine-leg clasps it in front of his face, his feet prancing balletically inches from the little wooden pickets. Beautiful.

7) BOOT HILL BOONY

Shane Warne's hat-trick victims at the MCG in '94 may have lacked a bit in the quality stakes, with Devon Malcolm following Gough and DeFreitas, but David Boon's diving grab off Dev's glove followed by that kitchen-sink celebration is worthy of any list.

6) CLEM'S BALLY FLUKE

It was 1902 at Old Trafford. England were floundering in pursuit of a modest target and needed eight more with two wickets left when England stumper Dick Lilley launched the ball out to square leg. Clem Hill, who was riding the boundary, picks up the story. "I raced after the ball with not the slightest idea of bringing off a catch, but with the full determination of saving a four. Almost on the boundary, after having run the best part of 25 yards, I threw everything to chance and made a dive at the leather. No one was more surprised than myself to find the ball stuck in my hand. Poor Dick Lilley passing me on the way to the pavilion said, 'Oh, Clem, what a bally fluke!' For appearances' sake I had to reply, 'Never on your life!' But the England wicketkeeper knew the truth and spoke it." Australia went on to win by three runs to take an unassailable lead in the series.

5) MILLER SAVES TAVARÉ'S BLUSHES

Fast-forward 80 years, to the fourth Test of the 1982/83 series at the MCG, and this time it was Australia chipping away at a target when a grab at the death would win the day. The Aussies should already have been dead and buried at 218 for 9 chasing 288, but Allan Border and Jeff Thomson refused to give it up, nurdling their way to within four of the target before Ian Botham sent down a wide long-hop. Thomson couldn't resist a nibble, guiding a gimme into – and out of – Chris Tavaré's mitts at second slip. To Tavaré's eternal relief, Geoff Miller was on hand to run round from first slip and scoop up the rebound. The celebrations began, and Tavaré was buying first drinks at the bar.

4) WALLY'S GRAB

Old Trafford, 1961, and England needed 256 in three-and-a-bit hours to take a 2-1 lead in the series with one to play. Ted Dexter fancied it was on and rattled along to 76. At 150 for 1 the hosts were cruising when Aussie skipper Richie Benaud pulled off another tactical masterstroke. With a damaged shoulder affecting his ability to spin the ball, he came round the wicket to the right-hander – then unheard of for a leggie – and focused on hitting the rough outside leg stump. The plan was perfect as Dexter attempted to cut a delivery that was a little too close to him and nicked it through to the great Wally Grout, who snaffled a stunner. England folded, Benaud finished with 6 for 70, and Australia took what proved to be a decisive lead in the series.

3) LANGER'S PREMATURE EXULTATION

Oh, how they wanted this one. After the blip of '05 the mangled mongrels of Australia were hot for revenge in '06, and at Brisbane Flintoff's England were immediately up against it, Ponting's redemptive century framing the early stages until Collingwood and Pietersen dragged the game late into the fourth day. Colly's dismissal brought Fred out, and after a couple of bunts, a short one from Warne was gut-churningly miscued to long-off, where Justin Langer and his black belt in arrogance were lurking. Just before the pill descended into his cruel and calloused martial-artist hands, the preening maniac awarded himself a clenched-fist celebration before actually catching the thing. It has a kind of Mourinho-like magnificence, provoking vast and deep swathes of hatred and love all at once. You'd have him in your side any day, the swine.

2) BERTIE FOUR FINGERS

Having bloodied the Aussies with the ball, Harold Larwood started slapping them about with the bat in the final Test of the 1932/33 Bodyline series, giving it some long-handle after coming in as nightwatchman. The Notts quick raced along to 98 until, on the threshold of a first Test century, he spooned the ball to long-on. To any other fielder it would have been a dolly, but underneath the ball was Bert "Dainty" Ironmonger – a 51-year-old missing a forefinger who, if he were still around today, would make Monty look like Jonty. Old Bert wasn't missing this one though, clinging on at ankle-height to deprive Larwood of a ton in what would prove to be his final Test. "The Australians clapped him all the way back to the pavilion," wrote Denzil Batchelor. "Either that, or they never stopped clapping Ironmonger for holding almost the only catch he ever held in his life."

1) FAMOUS STRAUSS

We all know it, but so what? No moment better captures the utter otherworldliness of that summer than Andrew Strauss and his

Newton-defying salmon-leap of faith. It was Fred from around the wicket, it was Gilchrist fencing away from his body, and it was Lord Brocket staying late in the office again, and the godlike Patrick Eagar snapping behind the lens. You can keep your Jones–Bowden–Richie heartstopper; *this* was perfection. ∎

Virender Sehwag's 201 not out at Galle accounted for 61 per cent of India's first-innings total

Lone Rangers

CRICKET: IT'S NOT REALLY
A TEAM GAME, IS IT?

10) NEWELL'S BLOCKADE
Warwickshire v Nottinghamshire, Edgbaston, 1988

Sometimes a player gets back in the dressing-room, surveys the debris and turns to his mates with a query along the lines of "What in Sir Garfield's name happened there, then?" So it was in 1988 when Mick Newell, Nottinghamshire grafter and now coach, returned to the away changing-room at Edgbaston, ten proud runs unbeaten, with no one else to play with. His heroic bat-carrying had occupied all of 22.2 overs as Notts were tumbled out for 44 (Gladstone Small 7 for 15). Amazingly, Newell's 10 not out is not the lowest score of its type in first-class history; that particular "honour" is reserved for Lancashire's RG Barlow, who fought his way to 5 not out in a two-hour knock against Notts in 1882.

9) FRED'S FURY
England v Sri Lanka, Lord's, 2006

As England captain Andrew Flintoff had a chequered time of it. A grand Johnny Cash-inspired win at Mumbai was forgotten amidst the late-night debris of the lost Ashes tour of 2006/07, and between these contrasting events Flintoff led his country at Lord's for the first and only time. After three days against Sri Lanka, Fred's tenure was looking rosy. But after asking Sri Lanka to follow on, he would endure two nightmarish days in the field as Mahela Jayawardene and friends occupied 199 overs to see out the match. Flintoff – at his best a hulking strike bowler but too often prepared to shoulder the donkey work – took it upon himself to get through 51 second-innings overs, making it 68 for the match. By the end of it his left ankle was shattered. He hobbled through two more Tests, before accepting the crutches.

8) BOTHAM SWEATS IT OUT
India v England, Mumbai, 1980

Forget all that 1981 stuff, Ian Botham's uncanniest impression of Atlas came at Mumbai in 1980. The scene was the one-off Golden Jubilee Test. In searing heat, the young hipster sent down 22 overs on the first day and snared six wickets. Then, in reply, England's top-order folded to 57 for 4, leaving Botham to rescue the innings with a blazing 114, scored from just 144 balls at a rate in excess of double that of his teammates. He hit 17 fours in all, as many as the rest of his team put together. Having powered England to a lead of 54, he again took the new ball, and in 26 overs ransacked a further seven wickets, giving him 13 in the match. The tourists had less than 100 to chase, and Beefy, having done his bit, could sniff out a beer.

7) VIRU-LENT VIOLENCE
Sri Lanka v India, Galle, 2008

Virender Sehwag's unique capacity to play a different game from everyone else makes him a must for this list. Of his 22 Test hundreds only eight fall below 150. He made four doubles and two triples, all scored at near to a run-a-ball. His most ridiculous solo act came against Sri Lanka in 2008, making 201 not out from a total of 329. Such is the way with genius, before the match he had told his teammates that he would get them a double-hundred and, as his garlanded mates succumbed to Murali and Mendis, Sehwag just batted as if it was a beer match, hitting 15 fours off the two spinners alone, to go with four merrily clumped sixes.

6) FIERY'S FALL
England v India, Headingley, 1967

Ah, Sir Geoffrey. It takes a special figure to spark an outcry after hitting a Test double-century. Boycott was not just out of form going into the 1967 series against India; he was also out of touch with the prevailing mood of selectors, media and watching public. On the first day of the series he crawled to 106 not out, having vowed to be there at the close, come what may. The following day – beneath the gathering clouds of a media storm that perceived a man playing more for himself than the team – Boycott hastened his scoring rate, hitting a further 140 in just under four hours, including a six, before his skipper and Yorkshire teammate Brian Close declared. The innings had taken up 555 balls and 10 hours, and his 246 not out would be the highest score of the summer in all first-class cricket. Close, who had showily put his arm around Boycott in the moment of declaration, later stated: "In different conditions, such tenacity would be hailed as a masterly exhibition of the bulldog spirit." But the masses, at least outside Headingley's terraces, were not happy. The selectors caught the mood, ostentatiously announcing after the Test had been completed (with a six-wicket win for England) that Boycott was to be dropped, not for slow scoring, but for the uglier sin of selfish batting. He would return again that summer, but uptight and confused, later admitting: "The stigma of being dropped by England, apparently for selfishness, was to mark the rest of my career."

5) FLOWER'S POWER
Zimbabwe v South Africa, Harare, 2001

England's former chieftain Andy Flower was once Test cricket's No.1-ranked batsman, reaching the summit while propping up lowly Zimbabwe. A regular one-man show during his playing days, he can lay claim to the most dominant individual performance in Test history. Flower began against South Africa at Harare in 2001 by keeping wicket for 139 overs, conceding not a single bye as the Proteas strolled to 600 for 3. Summoned to the middle in the 16th over of Zimbabwe's reply, he was last man out for 142. All out for 286, the home side followed on, and Flower was back in soon enough, this time repelling 470 balls to remain undefeated. On the pitch for all but 28 overs of the match, and in pads throughout, his second-innings 199 not out gave him 341 runs for once out: 50 per cent of his team's match total. And still Zimbabwe lost by nine wickets.

4) GIBSON & BROWN
Hampshire v Durham, Chester-le-Street, 2007

Two for one here: Hampshire and Durham's tussle in 2007 produced a first-rate lone crusader per side. To kick it off, Ottis Gibson took all 10 wickets for Durham in the first innings – the 79th player to achieve the feat. But throughout the carnage Hampshire opener Michael Brown was invincible, carrying his bat for an unbeaten 56 out of 115. He then went on to salvage an unlikely draw for Hampshire (who ended 262 for 9) with 126 not out.

3) CHAMPAGNE CHARLIE
Australia v England, 1st (ever) Test, MCG, 1877

Test cricket never looked so much like an individual sport as it did at the very beginning of time. While Charles Bannerman must have wondered where Test cricket had got its name, facing up to its first delivery and notching up 126 untroubled runs on the first day, the rest of the Australians fared rather less well, cobbling together 40 for 6 up to that point. The trailblazer retired hurt the next day with 165 to his name, probably feeling he'd done his share of the work; Bannerman's 67.3 per cent share of Australia's eventual 245 is still a record contribution for a completed Test innings. The next highest score made by an Aussie in the match was just 20, as Bannerman dragged his country to the first of many, many victories over poor old England.

2) HERCULEAN HADLEE
Australia v New Zealand, Brisbane, 1985

Rarely can one man have so completely dominated his national team for so long. Through the 1980s the Kiwis punched above their weight, beating the Windies at home and England and Australia away, and Richard Hadlee was the reason. A master of swing and seam and a superb competitor, a man who kept a list of his "career goals" pinned to the inside of his kit bag, Hadlee would blaze a trail to 400 Test wickets. His 15-wicket haul against the Aussies at Brisbane in 1985, setting up a series win against their oldest enemy, is still talked about as New Zealand's greatest individual performance.

1) LARA'S RECORD BLITZ
1994 county season

When Warwickshire nabbed the signature of Brian Lara in 1994 as a replacement for the injured and not-quite-so-sexy Manoj Prabhakar, it was like an already-decent pub team turning up on quiz night with Stephen Fry as a ringer. Lara had just taken 375 record-breaking runs off England and, after a few days' partying, staggered off a plane in chilly England straight into a Championship fixture against Glamorgan. Some 4,000 Brummies turned up at Edgbaston to see Lara hit 147, a knock under immense pressure that teammate Gladstone Small recalled as his best innings of the summer. It would have some competition. Next up was Leicestershire, captained by Lara's West Indian pal Phil Simmons. Lara made a pair of hundreds to ensure a draw. He then stroked 136 against Somerset, bringing him his fifth first-class century in a row. Although he was strangled down the leg side against Middlesex going for the record-equalling sixth, Lara was undeterred, and took guard against Durham the following week with an eye on something special. Small recalls a chat at lunch on the final day between Lara and Warwickshire's captain Dermot Reeve, who'd been weighing up a declaration. Lara was on 297 at the time. "Will you let me go for the record?" was the gist of it. Four hours later, to the penultimate ball of the match, Lara clattered his 62nd four through the covers to become the first man to break the 500-run barrier. In all that summer he would make nine tons, 2,066 runs, take the Man of the Match award in the B&H Cup final and inspire Warwickshire to their first Championship since 1972. ∎

Mohammad Azharuddin's tour de force at Lord's was overshadowed by Graham Gooch

Forgotten Gems

THE GREATEST INNINGS EVER TO HAVE BEEN MISSED, OVERSHADOWED OR CRIMINALLY UNREMEMBERED

10) JONES HELPS FRED

Simon Jones: 12*, England v Australia, 2nd Test, Edgbaston, 2005

When a game is won by a handful of runs, we inevitably look to extras, untaken singles and fumbles in the field for our "what if" pub chats. When Edgbaston 2005 comes up – and it does, a lot – few acknowledge the role of Simon Jones, other than a shelled catch at third man as the game entered its unhinged conclusion. Warne had just claimed his fourth and fifth wickets of the innings when Jones joined Andrew Flintoff on 131 for 9, with England looking to set Australia a tricky fourth-innings target. Jones negotiated the hat-trick ball (hitting the following ball for four!) and went on to score 12 of a last-wicket stand of 51, giving the visitors a 282-run target. Correct us if we're wrong, but we don't think they quite reached it.

9) THE OLD ONES ARE THE BEST

Chris Old: 29, England v Australia, 3rd Test, Headingley, 1981

There are lots of things everyone remembers about Headingley '81. Brearley's return, Botham's 149 not out, his jumper and his cigar, Big Bob's 8 for 43, the young blond Dilley's dashing maiden half-century (56). But equally crucial on that legendary fourth evening when England built an unlikely but ultimately telling lead was the second support act offered by Yorkshire quick Chris Old, whose 29 from No.10 came in a partnership of 67 alongside Sir Beef. Old was primarily a skilful outswing bowler, but he also made six first-class hundreds, fielded in the slips, captained his county, and one cloudy afternoon in July on his home ground played his own vital part in English cricket's greatest folk tale.

8) SLINGS AND ARROWS
Thilan Samaraweera: 214, Pakistan v Sri Lanka, 2nd Test, Lahore, 2009

The second match of this Test series at the Gaddafi Stadium marks the last time Pakistan played a Test match in front of a home crowd. As the Sri Lankan team made their way to the ground for the third day, their bus came under fire. Of the players to be injured, Thilan Samaraweera came off worst as a bullet penetrated 12 inches into his left thigh. Less than 24 hours earlier, he was out in the middle celebrating a well-constructed double-ton, having also scored 231 in the previous match at Karachi. Samaraweera spent the next three months wondering whether he would recover – physically and mentally – for a return to professional sport. He did later return to make his 50th Test appearance and went on to pass 1,000 runs for the calendar year for the first time in his career.

7) CLASS HARV FULL
Neil Harvey: 151*, South Africa v Australia, 3rd Test, Durban, 1950

This match is remembered almost entirely for the decision, taken by Dudley Nourse, not to enforce the follow-on, as he became the first captain to choose not to and still lose. In fairness to him, it is impossible to legislate for a batsman in such supreme form as Neil Harvey was. Chasing 336, on a pitch that was turning square, and on which the previous two innings tallied 176 in total, Harvey danced his way to 151 match-winning, chanceless runs, taking South Africa's greatest spinner Hugh Tayfield – fresh off 7 for 23 in the first dig – to the cleaners in the process. Wisden later described the innings as "literally flawless".

6) IF THE GAFFER MADE A TON IN AN EMPTY STADIUM, DID IT REALLY HAPPEN?

Alec Stewart: 123, England v Sri Lanka, 3rd Test, Old Trafford, 2002

When, as a much-loved veteran, you stroke your way to a classy 123 from 190 balls to see your side to upwards of 500 in the first dig, you'd generally expect a decent reception. But when Stewie passed three figures on the third morning in Manchester, taking four balls to move from 86 to 102, there was barely a soul there to see it. They'd all poured out from their seats to catch the England football team's second-round World Cup tie against Denmark in Japan. It evoked memories of Old Trafford in 1998, when Robert Croft and Angus Fraser took the plaudits for a dramatic draw against South Africa, after captain Stewart had made a brilliant and crucial 164 earlier in the day.

5) KING'S AT LORD'S

Collis King: 86, England v West Indies, World Cup final, Lord's, 1979

With his glazed eyes and long handle, Collis King loped out to join Viv with the Windies in trouble. England had knocked four away for 99 when King joined the king. The great man himself was struggling as England's schemers Hendrick, Botham and Old applied the strangle. It needed Collis to let loose and when Boycott came on, round the wicket with his cap on, looking to dob it on a length, he went postal, peppering the Tavern Stand with proto-IPL disregard for the occasion and the boundary rope. Viv relaxed, and when Collis departed with his 86 from 66 having changed the complexion of the match, the master took over on his way to 138 not out. Collis sloped off soon after, rarely playing again for West Indies. Job done.

4) JIMMY CRICKET

Jimmy Adams: 94, West Indies v Australia, 2nd Test, Jamaica, 1999

It suits Jimmy Adams that his most significant Test innings was completely overshadowed. With West Indies at one of their lowest ebbs, he prodded and blocked his way magnificently to 94 as Brian Lara piled up 213 tide-shifting runs at the other end against the greatest team in the world. The match and series may belong to Lara alone, but without Adams' unassuming grit it could never have been. It is almost better that he was dismissed six short of a ton, lest he stole any of the limelight for himself.

3) SOME PRING SPECIAL
Derek Pringle: 27, England v West Indies, 1st Test, Headingley, 1991

In his light-blue lid, XXL sweater and toothpick Duncan Fearnley bat, Suggs stood resolute at the other end as Graham Gooch – his teammate for England and Essex – took on the might of Marshall and his pack. It was dark at Headingley, the clouds dank with the weight of history – England had not won a home Test against West Indies since 1969. Gooch was on course to play one of Test cricket's great innings, an authentic annals-botherer, carrying his SS for 154 not out from 252 all out. But without Pring's weirdly impudent and utterly English 27 from a partnership of 98 for the seventh wicket, the legend of Leeds and the grandeur of Gooch would never have come to pass.

2) MO'S MASTERPIECE
Mohammad Azharuddin: 121, England v India, 1st Test, Lord's, 1990

The monstrous heft of Gooch's triple-century dominated the patrons of NW8 to such a terrifying extent that what followed felt like a back-alley peep show compared to the captain's Last Night at the Proms. Yet in truth his opposite number – in his olive-green helmet and dangling Taweez amulet, all wrists and feet and Pacino shrugs – played the game's truly masterful knock. Azharuddin, India's captain, leant back to crash half-volleys off the back foot, whipped short wide ones through square leg and climbed into the 41-year-old Eddie Hemmings with a chutzpah rarely seen at Lord's. His 88-ball hundred lit up the Saturday, before nice guy Eddie got his man with a ripper through the gate. One of the great lost innings at HQ; Gooch may have taken the title, but Azhar got the girl.

1) STAN THE MAN BEATS BODYLINE

Stan McCabe: 187*, Australia v England, 1st Test, SCG, 1932

In the most famous series of all, dashing 22-year-old Aussie strokemaker Stan McCabe made a miraculous early impression. The Don wasn't playing the first Test, but McCabe's 187 at Sydney was a masterpiece that quickly got buried under all the Bodyline bolshiness. It has been scandalously consigned to the margins ever since, pushed out by Bradman-mania and the creeping mythologising of Jardine and his attack-dog, the searingly quick Harold Larwood. It's a shame that the cult of personality wins out over a wiry man with glistening cheekbones and sunken eyes who can play one of Test cricket's greatest and bravest innings and yet be largely forgotten because he's not a ready-made icon. ∎

Albert Trott hit
a long ball

Memorable Sixes

HELLO, MASSIVE!

10) "I WANT TO HIT A SIX NOW"

Virender Sehwag could have been forgiven a few nerves as he moved to within five runs of becoming the first Indian to score a Test triple, with his idol standing at the non-striker's end. But then Viru's mind has never really worked like that. "When I was on 295, before Saqlain Mushtaq bowled, I told Sachin that whether it was slow, fast or whatever, I would step out and hit him for six," Sehwag said in 2014. "Whatever will happen, will happen. I don't care, I want to hit a six now." And that's what he did, taking two steps down the wicket and launching Saqlain over cow to bring up Test cricket's fastest triple-century. He'd break his own record four years later.

9) HOT TO TROTT

Forget your talk of big bats; it's all about the motion in the ocean. Back in 1899, Albert Trott smashed Monty Noble over the Lord's pavilion and into the racquet courts. Bosh. It was the first time such a hit had ever been achieved – and it hasn't been replicated. Not by Gayle, not by Viv, not by Afridi. Judging by an interview with *Boy's Own*, Trott was pretty chuffed with his efforts. "Noble was bowling, and sending the balls down in pretty good style, and at last I struck at one. I was not very sure about it; and the next thing I saw was the ball looking like a pea in the air, and I learned then that it had just touched a chimney and nearly gone out of the ground." Noble had him caught at third-man soon after attempting another big 'un so he's the real winner.

8) THE FULL MONTY

Much-maligned with the bat was Monty Panesar. He'd invariably play three very pretty blocks, then miss the fourth. That's probably the reason he averaged under 5 in Tests. There was one highpoint – higher even than the Cardiff and Auckland draws – with the willow, and that came in 2006. He was facing Murali, England were nine down, in a post-2005 slump, and on the verge of another defeat. What did Monty do? Bat like a dream and slog-sweep his only Test maximum. You can imagine how the fake beards in the crowd reacted to that one.

7) BOOM BOOM BANGS THE ROOF

Power Cricket, they called it. It was at the Millennium Stadium in 2002 and the world of cricket was about to change. All the stars were in – Shoaib Akhtar, Courtney Walsh, Wasim Akram... Matthew Fleming – and the 75,000-seater stadium had only 71,000 empty seats on the opening night. Played indoors, and with additional runs for hitting the ball into the middle tier (8), top tier (10) or onto the roof (12), history was made when Shahid Afridi muscled a Fleming delivery skyward and it came back down off the old rain-stopper. Umpire Vanburn Holder did a weird new signal that's not been seen since – his raised wrist-cross looks like he's demanding justice for a jailed comrade – and the world smiled. It's classic Afridi, of course, a man who once smashed Ryan McLaren 158 metres. Look it up, it's massive.

6) WHERE THERE'S KAPIL, THERE'S A WAY

With India 430 for 9 in reply to England's 653, veteran skipper and swashbuckling all-rounder Kapil Dev – in at

No.8 – needed to somehow get 24 runs to avoid the follow-on, with leg-spinner and old-school bunny No.11 Narendra Hirwani up the other end. Eddie Hemmings arrived at the Nursery End for an over of airy off-spin, and Kapil saw his chance, swinging four successive sixes back over the roly-poly twirler's head before turning, laughing, to his teammates on the balcony and performing an understated fist-pump. As Richie Benaud mused on commentary, "Well, I suppose it's only logical, if you need 24 to save the follow-on, why wouldn't you get it in four hits?" Kapil was justified: Hirwani was out next ball.

5) SOBERS' SIX SQUARED

Garry Sobers, captain of Nottinghamshire, was facing Glamorgan's Malcolm Nash at St Helen's, Swansea. Nash, a left-arm seamer, was experimenting with spin. Sobers swung wildly from the hip and – with help from a short boundary and a catch carried over the line at long-off for the fifth – became the first man to hit six sixes in an over. And thank heavens, they were filming the thing. The beleaguered ball itself has been the subject of debate – the first and sixth hits were sent out of the ground and Nash has since questioned whether the ball exhibited and sold at auction is the self-same pill that Sobers sent flying down the King Edward Road back in '68.

4) SON OF A SWITCH

The reverse-sweep? Fine. Newfangled, but fine. But jumping round, switching hands, becoming a left-hander and still smashing it out of the ground? Ridiculous. Unfair, said some. Kevin Pietersen started it (initially against spin) to Murali in a Test at Edgbaston in 2006, and then again against seam (albeit the medium-pace of Scott Styris) twice in an ODI at Chester-le-Street the following year. Truly a game-changer and a debate-inspirer. Who'd have thought that from Pietersen?

3) WELL BATTED, DARLING

Until 1910 a six was only awarded if the ball was hit out of the ground, which perhaps explains why it took 55 matches before anyone achieved the feat in Test cricket. The first man to do so, in 1898, was a double-hard Aussie by the delightful name of Joe Darling. He picked a fine time to do it, belting the great English left-arm spinner Johnny Briggs over the eastern gate and into a nearby car park at the Adelaide Oval to bring up his century.

2) GAYLE HITS GAZI OFF THE STRIP

It took 2,057 matches before anyone had the audacity to whack the first ball of a Test over the boundary ropes, and it came as no great surprise that the man with the reportedly often ill-concealed cojones to do it was Chris Gayle. Long-form cricket has become an unfamiliar and often-confusing beast to the Jamaican in recent years, so he thought it best to stick to what he knows and keep trying to put the ball in the stands. Gayle shimmied down the track to Bangladesh off-spinner Sohag Gazi's first delivery and deposited the shell-shocked debutant over long-on. That Gazi dismissed him four overs later was largely forgotten as Gayle retired to the changing-room with 24 from 17 deliveries and a small slice of history.

1) CAPTAIN COOL SEALS THE DEAL

A World Cup on the line, 35,000 screaming fans crammed into the Wankhede, another 135 million Indians watching at home, not to mention many millions more around the world, and the hopes of the nation rest on your shoulders. No pressure, MS. With India stuttering in their chase of 275, their out-of-nick captain decides to promote himself to No.5. "Something in me said I should go," Dhoni later said. "I knew in my heart it was justified and felt that the team trusted me." That trust was repaid as Dhoni produced a nerveless 91 not out, thumping Nuwan Kulasekara over long-on to complete the win with a six that rang out across the world. ∎

England's Greatest Uncapped Players

POWERHOUSES OF THE COUNTY GAME WHO
NEVER GOT A CRACK AT TEST CRICKET, NO MATTER
HOW HARD THEY BANGED ON THE DOOR

10) PETER ROEBUCK (SOMERSET)

A defensively-minded opener, former Somerset skipper Roebuck made 17,558 runs with 33 first-class hundreds but was prone to bouts of crippling intensity that held him back as a batsman. Roebuck later became a trenchant journalist and radio broadcaster, and his post-retirement story, in particular the mysterious circumstances surrounding his sudden death at a Cape Town hotel in 2011, significantly overshadowed his feats as a player.

9) GEOFF HUMPAGE (WARWICKSHIRE)

A legendary Warwickshire stumper, Humpage's bearded brilliance lit up Edgbaston through the 1970s and '80s. In many ways ahead of his time, he was a meaty middle-order hitter who struck 29 first-class hundreds in an era when runs from keepers were considered a bonus. He did play three ODIs but that was as good as it got, and his presence on the 1982 rebel tour effectively kyboshed any lingering hopes of a Test call-up. He became a copper after retiring in 1990.

8) MAL LOYE (NORTHAMPTONSHIRE AND LANCASHIRE)

When Loye scored nearly 1,200 first-class runs in 1998, and earned himself the PCA Cricketer of the Year Award, he seemed set for an international career. In fact, he came so close that ahead of England's one-off Test against Sri Lanka at the end of that year he was wrongly told he'd be making his debut. A heavy scorer in county cricket, Loye had to settle for some England "A" caps and a short-lived but memorable ODI career when in 2007 he took to one knee and slog-swept Brett Lee for six.

7) ALI BROWN (SURREY AND NOTTINGHAMSHIRE)

With 26,898 first-class runs at 42.67, Brown was a distinguished No.5 in the four-day format. In one-day cricket he was a boldly aggressive opener, whose 16 ODIs did not do justice to his ability, despite him making 118 in only his third appearance. Brown's 268 from 160 balls for Surrey against Glamorgan in 2002 remains the highest score in the history of one-day cricket. He wasn't just a one-day crowd-pleaser, though. His 47 first-class centuries suggest a talent that should not have been overlooked by England's Test selectors.

6) PETER SAINSBURY (HAMPSHIRE)

The only man to play in both of Hampshire's Championship-winning sides in 1961 and '73, Sainsbury was a genuine all-rounder who was unfortunate to play in a golden era of English spinners. His slow left-armers, always probing but rarely turning extravagantly, were good enough to take over 50 wickets in a season 15 times. But ahead of him throughout his career were Underwood, Illingworth, Lock and Titmus. He was also strong enough with the bat to score 1,000 runs in a season on six occasions.

5) TREVOR JESTY (HAMPSHIRE, SURREY AND LANCASHIRE)

Just ten ODIs were the sum international opportunity afforded to Jesty, an energetic all-rounder boasting 35 hundreds and 19 five-fers in first-class cricket. Eight of those tons came in 1982, his best year with Hampshire, when he made 1,645 at 58.75 from No.4 as well as taking 35 wickets at 21 with his medium-pace. Even after that return, he was left out of the winter's Ashes touring party under England captain Bob Willis – a man whose Warwickshire side Jesty would take for a 64-minute 134 in the final game of the Championship season two days after the squad was announced.

4) GLEN CHAPPLE (LANCASHIRE)

Up in Lancashire, the fact that Chapple has never played Test cricket is as lamented as the rain. The seamer has got the better of batsmen in domestic cricket since 1992 and is only 15 first-class wickets shy of 1,000. His haul of 6 for 18 in the 1996 NatWest Trophy final and his efforts in 2011 to help his county win their first outright County Championship title since 1934 were roundly praised, but that elusive England Test cap never came. He did represent his country once, in an ODI against Ireland in 2006, but injury limited him to just four overs.

3) ALAN JONES (GLAMORGAN)

A colossus at Glamorgan for more than a quarter of a century, Jones topped 1,000 runs in 23 consecutive seasons between 1961 and '83. He can consider himself particularly unfortunate not to have earned a Test cap given that he represented England in a five-day match not given official Test status, against a Rest of the World XI in 1970. Described as a "fundamentally correct and determined" left-handed opener by John Arlott, Jones had two stints as Glamorgan skipper and was the archetypal county pro. No batsman has scored more first-class runs without playing Test cricket.

2) TONY NICHOLSON (YORKSHIRE)

Dickie Bird called Nicholson "the unluckiest player not to play for England", and he has a strong case. His stats – 879 wickets at 19.76

– make for impressive reading and he was integral to the Yorkshire side that dominated the 1960s, taking 113 wickets at 15.50 in 1966. Still that wasn't enough for England. He had been selected a couple of years earlier for the 1964/65 tour to South Africa, but his fleeting opportunity was ended by injury.

1) DON SHEPHERD (GLAMORGAN)

No bowler has taken more first-class wickets than Shepherd without winning a Test cap. To Glamorgan supporters, this was nothing short of a travesty, and his record suggests they weren't far wide of the mark. In a career spanning 22 years, Shepherd took 2,218 first-class wickets at a touch over 21. Initially a fast-medium bowler, a drop in form led him to switch to medium-pace off-cutters in 1956 and, after a superb campaign in which he took 177 wickets at 15, he never looked back. He was Glamorgan's talisman in their Championship title win in 1969 and one of *Wisden*'s Cricketers of the Year in 1970. ∎

A haul of more than 2,000 first-class wickets wasn't enough to earn Don Shepherd a Test cap

Len Hutton passing
on his expertise to his
son Richard

Dynasties

IT'S A FAMILY AFFAIR

10) THE WAUGHS

Steve Waugh First-class matches: 356 (1984–2004) Tests: 168 (1985–2004)
Mark Waugh First-class matches: 368 (1985–2004) Tests: 128 (1991–2002)
Dean Waugh First-class matches: 1 (1995)

The Waugh twins were the heartbeat of the Australian middle order throughout the Nineties, as Steve (gritty, dogged) and Mark (laconic, mulleted) combined to great effect. Steve was the first to receive his Baggy Green, making his debut against India in 1985. Mark, the younger sibling by four minutes, and thus fated to be known as Junior for the rest of his days, had to wait a further six years for his first taste of Test cricket.

When Junior did eventually receive the call during the 1991 Ashes, hitting a stunning debut hundred at Adelaide, it was a bittersweet experience, coming as it did at the expense of Steve's place in the side. Steve went on to become the most successful captain in Australia's history while the mercurial Mark cemented his place at No.4 for the next decade but continued to thrill and frustrate in equal measure. Between them they defined modern Australian cricket – guts, drive, grit; style, elegance, class.

Younger brother Dean also had a brief first-class career but, if the opinion of ex-New South Wales paceman Richard Stobo is anything to go by, he wasn't quite in the same league as his more celebrated brothers. After beating Dean's outside edge several times in succession during a Sydney grade game, an exasperated Stobo exclaimed, "For Christ's sake, Dean, you must have been f*****g adopted." More recently, Steve's son Austin has picked up the family baton, hitting a century for Metro New South Wales in the 2016 final of the national under-17 championships.

9) THE HUSSAINS
Joe Hussain First-class matches: 1 (1964)
Mel Hussain First-class matches: 1 (1985)
Nasser Hussain First-class matches: 334 (1987–2004) Tests: 96 (1990–2004)

Jawad Hussain – or Joe, as the lads who came to his famous Ilford Cricket School knew him – passed away in April 2008. He was 68. He left behind two cricketing sons. His eldest boy, Mel, played a single first-class game for Worcestershire before moving successfully into the business world; the other, Nasser, you may have heard of.

Joe himself played a single game for Madras in India before starting a new life in England, taking over the rickety old cricket school in Ilford and turning it into a breeding ground for future Essex cricketers. Graham Gooch, John Lever and Ravi Bopara are just a few of the names to have passed through its doors, but it was more than just a finishing school for budding professionals; Joe's place was a *haven* for cricket. It gave young lads – many from the cricketing no-man's-land of east London and its outskirts – a rare chance to swing a bat or spin a ball.

Joe gave us Nasser, and all that flowed from him. That is legacy enough. But for every Nasser, Goochie or Ravi, there were another hundred nippers who walked through those doors knowing nothing, and who walked out knowing so much more.

8) THE COWDREYS
Ernest Cowdrey First-class matches: 1 (1926)
Colin Cowdrey First-class matches: 692 (1950–76) Tests: 114 (1954–75)
Chris Cowdrey First-class matches: 299 (1977–92) Tests: 6 (1984–88)
Graham Cowdrey First-class matches: 179 (1984–97)
Fabian Cowdrey First-class matches: 12 (2013–)

In 1934 a cricket-mad father named Ernest taught his son, christened with the initials MCC, to play with a straight bat while practising on a tennis court in south India. It was a lesson well learned.

Thirty-four years later Michael Colin Cowdrey walked out to bat at Edgbaston in his 100th Test match, becoming the first cricketer to reach the milestone. He marked the occasion in style by scoring his 21st Test century. Cowdrey played 114 Tests and averaged 44, and it's testament to his ability that, despite such achievements, Fred Trueman once described him as "a terrific talent who never fulfilled his potential."

Enter his two sons, Chris and Graham. No pressure.

A solid county all-rounder for Kent and later Glamorgan, Chris's big moment came in 1988 when he was unexpectedly made captain of England against West Indies. With his godfather Peter May as chairman of selectors and a modest county record behind him, nepotism was shouted from the rooftops. Cowdrey scored 0 and 5, West Indies romped home by 10 wickets, and he never played for his country again.

Younger brother Graham enjoyed a long career at Kent as a hard-hitting middle-order batsman and in 1995 shared a partnership of 368 with Aravinda de Silva, which remains a record for any wicket for the county.

In 2013 the latest chapter in the Cowdrey story began as Chris's son Fabian made his debut for Kent.

7) THE HUTTONS

Sir Leonard Hutton First-class matches: 513 (1934–55) Tests: 79 (1937–55)
Ben Brocklehurst First-class matches: 64 (1952–54)
Frank Dennis First-class matches: 92 (1928–39)
Richard Hutton First-class matches: 281 (1962–76) Tests: 5 (1971)
John Hutton First-class matches: 1 (1973)
Simon Dennis First-class matches: 104 (1980–91)
Ben Hutton First-class matches: 110 (1998–2007)
Oliver Hutton First-class matches: 1 (2004)

Arguably the greatest batsman England has ever produced, none of Sir Leonard's relations came close to matching his achievements, but for sheer numbers and family connections the Huttons rate as one of cricket's most impressive dynasties.

Len played 79 Tests and would have played many more but for the War. In 1938 the Yorkshire-born opening batsman surpassed Wally Hammond's world-record Test score, making 364 against Australia at The Oval.

Len played county cricket alongside his brother-in-law, the fast bowler Frank Dennis, who had a long and successful spell with Yorkshire. And to continue the family connection, Frank's nephew Simon played over 100 first-class matches during the Eighties for Yorkshire and Glamorgan.

Len's two sons John and Richard also went on to play first-class cricket. John played just one match for MCC but older brother Richard had a more decorated career, spending 12 years at Yorkshire and playing five Test matches for England. In 1971 Richard was selected to play for the World XI that replaced the South African tourists in Australia, but alongside some of the greats of Test cricket he looked out of his depth and subsequently faded into international obscurity.

The most recent generation of Huttons to have played professional cricket are Len's two grandsons Oliver and Ben. Younger brother Oliver represented Oxford University, while Ben spent 10 years at Middlesex captaining the side for two seasons before retiring in 2007.

As though Ben and Oliver's cricketing heritage wasn't extensive enough, their other grandfather was the late Ben Brocklehurst, a former Somerset captain and proprietor of *The Cricketer* magazine, a publication later edited by Richard Hutton.

6) THE POLLOCKS

Andrew Pollock First-class matches: 7 (1934–38)
Robert Howden First-class matches: 3 (1939–40)
Peter Pollock First-class matches: 127 (1958–72) Tests: 28 (1961–70)
Graeme Pollock First-class matches: 262 (1960–87) Tests: 23 (1963–70)
Andrew Pollock First-class matches: 21 (1991–98)
Anthony Pollock First-class matches: 33 (1991–2000)
Shaun Pollock First-class matches: 186 (1991–2008) Tests: 108 (1995–2008)

Peter and Graeme Pollock were two of the very finest of the unlucky generation of South African cricketers to have their Test careers curtailed. The South African tour to England in 1965 left observers in little doubt of their talent as the Pollock brothers inspired their team to a victory at Trent Bridge that led to a series win. But this was to be the pair's only tour to England as South Africa's ban from international cricket followed in 1971.

The siblings had a considerable cricketing pedigree, with their father Andrew keeping wicket for Orange Free State and their uncle Robert Howden representing Natal in the Thirties. And the family of professional cricketers kept growing as Graeme's sons, Andrew and Anthony, both went on to represent Easterns, Transvaal and Leicestershire. But it was Peter's son Shaun who was the star of the next Pollock generation.

Shaun will be remembered as one of the modern game's great all-rounders and his 108-Test career must have offered some consolation to his father, whose own Test career was cut short after just 28 matches.

5) THE HADLEES
Walter Hadlee First-class matches: 117 (1933–52) Tests: 11 (1937–51)
Barry Hadlee First-class matches: 84 (1961–81)
Dayle Hadlee First-class matches: 111 (1966–84) Tests: 26 (1969–78)
Sir Richard Hadlee First-class matches: 342 (1971–90) Tests: 86 (1973–90)

Cricket is something of a family business in New Zealand. With a population of four-and-a-half million and just six first-class teams, it would seem the right genetic make-up puts you on the fast track to international recognition. Cairns, Crowe, Howarth, Bracewell and Harris have all been recurring names for the Black Caps, and in recent years the Marshalls, McCullums, Lathams, Rutherfords and Redmonds have kept the family tradition alive. But the honour of New Zealand's undisputed cricketing royal family must surely go to the Hadlees.

The legacy began with Walter Hadlee, an opening batsman who captained New Zealand on their tour of England in 1949. Still seeking their first Test victory, he led the relative international newcomers to a creditable 0-0 series draw. Walter played 11 Tests and went on to play a key role in the administration of New Zealand cricket as a national selector, team manager and chairman of the board. But his most valuable contribution to New Zealand cricket was his offspring.

The first to make the breakthrough was pace bowler Dayle, but even Hadlee senior wasn't convinced. "They got the wrong Hadlee," declared Walter, believing the selectors should have opted for older brother Barry instead. Despite his old man's protestations, Dayle went on to have a respectable international career, taking 71 wickets in 26 Tests.

Elder brother Barry did eventually make his international bow at the age of 33. An opening batsman in the mould of his father, he featured in two ODIs alongside his brothers, Dayle and Richard.

If Walter was the first king of New Zealand cricket then Richard was his undisputed heir. In an international career spanning 17 years he took the national team to unprecedented heights, becoming the first player to take 400 wickets in Test cricket and scoring over 3,000 runs for good measure.

4) THE CHAPPELLS
Vic Richardson First-class matches: 184 (1918–38) Tests: 19 (1924–36)
Ian Chappell First-class matches: 262 (1961–80) Tests: 75 (1964–80)
Greg Chappell First-class matches: 321 (1966–84) Tests: 87 (1970–84)
Trevor Chappell First-class matches: 88 (1972–85) Tests: 3 (1981)

The win-at-all-costs attitude that became synonymous with Australian cricket can in large part be credited to the Chappell dynasty. Vic Richardson, the grandfather of the Chappell triumvirate, was a fierce competitor and remarkable all-round sportsman. An exceptional fielder and destructive middle-order batsman, he played 19 Test matches for Australia between 1924 and '36, captaining his country on five occasions.

Some of the old man's talent rubbed off and his two eldest grandsons, Ian and Greg, will be remembered as two of the greatest players ever to done the Baggy Green. Famously described by John Arlott as "a cricketer of effect rather than the graces", Ian was as tenacious and tempestuous as they come. Often acknowledged as the architect of sledging, "Chappelli" was more than happy to put a few noses out of joint to aid the Australian cause. He later said: "As a captain of Australia my philosophy was simple: between 11am and 6pm there was no time to be a nice guy. We didn't deliberately set out to be a bunch of bastards but I'd much prefer to be described like that than a nice bunch of blokes on the field."

Ian's younger brother Greg didn't reach the same heights as captain of the national side, but he was the superior Australian batsman of his generation, averaging 54 in his 87-Test career.

Baby brother Trevor never fully stepped from the shadow of his brothers. Despite playing three Tests and 20 ODIs, the bowling all-rounder will be best remembered for his role in the infamous underarm incident, after older brother Greg instructed him to roll the ball along the ground to ensure victory in an ODI against New Zealand in 1981.

3) THE HEADLEYS

George Headley First-class matches: 103 (1927–54) Tests: 22 (1930–54)
Ron Headley First-class matches: 423 (1958–74) Tests: 2 (1973)
Dean Headley First-class matches: 139 (1991–99) Tests: 15 (1997–99)

The Headley dynasty makes the record books by virtue of being the only family to have had three generations play Test cricket. It started with Panama-born George, who went on to become one of the greatest ever Test batsmen. However, the dynasty could have been halted before it had even begun but for a fateful intervention.

George, who moved to Jamaica aged 10, had planned to pursue a career in dentistry in the USA but, while waiting for a delayed passport, he was selected to play against a visiting English team. The gifted right-hander scored 78 and 211 in consecutive matches and a star was born. Dubbed "The Black Bradman", he went on to become the first great batsman to emerge from the Caribbean, scoring 176 on his Test debut against England in 1930. In a career punctuated by the World War II, Headley played 22 Tests and hit ten centuries at an average of over 60. "I recognised quite early that you can't have two geniuses – father and son – in one family," said George's son Ron. "I felt annoyance at other people as they would try and compare me with him."

Nonetheless, left-handed opener Ron spent 16 seasons at Worcestershire and was a key member of the side that won back-to-back Championships in 1964 and '65. In the twilight of his career he received the call he thought would never come when he was drafted into the West Indies Test side to play England in 1973 after an injury crisis, but his best years were already behind him and he played just two matches with little success.

His son Dean enjoyed a more successful international career. After languishing in Middlesex's second XI and struggling to make an impact after a move to Kent, he announced himself in 1996 with three hat-tricks in a season. The following year he made his England debut against Australia at Manchester. The right-arm paceman gave Australia's left-handers a torrid time and took eight wickets in the match. He repeated his feats in the 1998/99 Ashes series, taking 6 for 60 in the second innings at Melbourne to scoop the Man of the Match award and give England a famous victory. However, like his father, he never fulfilled his potential in Test cricket as his career was curtailed after just 15 Tests when he was forced to retire in 1999 with persistent back problems.

2) THE MOHAMMADS

Wazir Mohammad First-class matches: 105 (1949–64) Tests: 20 (1952–59)
Raees Mohammad First-class matches: 30 (1948–63)
Hanif Mohammad First-class matches: 238 (1951–76) Tests: 55 (1952–69)
Mushtaq Mohammad First-class matches: 502 (1956–80) Tests: 57 (1959–79)
Sadiq Mohammad First-class matches: 387 (1960–85) Tests: 41 (1969–81)
Shoaib Mohammad First-class matches: 211 (1976–2002) Tests: 45 (1983–1995)

No other dynasty has had such an impact on the shaping of a cricketing nation than that of the Mohammads. Following Pakistan's introduction to Test cricket in 1952, the first 101 Tests they played featured a member of the Mohammad family.

Four brothers – Wazir, Hanif, Mushtaq and Sadiq – played a total of 170 Tests for Pakistan, and a fifth brother, Raees, was told the night before a Test match that he was selected, only to be demoted to twelfth man the following morning.

Hanif was the star of the family. Renowned for his unparalleled powers of concentration, he retains the record for the longest innings in Test history for his 337 in 970 minutes against West Indies in 1958. The following year he achieved the then-highest first-class innings, scoring 499 for Karachi.

His son Shoaib went on to enjoy a successful Test career, scoring seven centuries in 45 matches and proving to be a key figure as Pakistan made their mark on the world stage in the 1980s.

1) THE GRACES
Edward Grace First-class matches: 314 (1862–96) Tests: 1 (1880)
WG Grace First-class matches: 870 (1865–1908) Tests: 22 (1880–99)
Fred Grace First-class matches: 195 (1866–80) Tests: 1 (1880)
Henry Grace First-class matches: 3 (1871)
WG Grace (jnr) First-class matches: 57 (1893–1903)
Charles Grace First-class matches: 4 (1900–06)
Alfred Grace First-class matches: 2 (1886–1891)
Norman Grace First-class matches: 3 (1920–27)

In 1848, in Downend, Bristol, Martha Grace gave birth to the third of four sons. She christened him William Gilbert. WG – or Gilbert as Martha called him – was born into cricket. His father Henry and his uncle Alfred were enthusiasts, but it was Martha, in the family's back garden around the vegetable patch, who is said to have taught the game to her children. All her boys showed aptitude, with WG showing particular promise.

Martha was sport's first pushy parent. In 1859 she wrote to George Parr, the England captain, with an audacious request: "I am writing to ask you to consider the inclusion of my son, EM Grace – a splendid hitter and most excellent catch – in your England XI. I am sure he would play very well and do the team much credit. It may interest you to learn that I have a younger son, now 12 years of age, who will in time be a much better player than his brother because his back stroke is sounder, and he always plays with a straight bat. His name is WG Grace."

Edward would indeed go on to play for England, as would younger son Fred, but they would be usurped by their middle sibling. What is most revealing from the letter is the reference to her young son's back-foot technique and straight bat; WG was later credited as the first player to play off both front and back foot.

CLR James asserts in *Beyond a Boundary* that WG Grace was a towering figure who was personally responsible for popularising the game, nothing less than the most famous and iconic Englishman of the Victorian era. Without Martha's enthusiasm, the game would not be what it is today. God bless Mother Cricket. ■

Irresistible Comebacks

THEY THOUGHT IT WAS ALL OVER...

10) FRED TITMUS
Middlesex v Surrey, Lord's, 1982

Having lost four toes to a boat driven by Penny Cowdrey – wife of then England captain Colin – and having retired from the game six years previously, Fred Titmus probably wasn't the bookies' favourite to take the match-winning wicket in this Championship game. But the pitch was dry and crumbling and Mike Brearley asked the 49-year-old if he could help out, so he muscled in on the spin-twin pairing of Edmonds and Emburey to make three a magic number and nab 3 for 43 to win the match for his team.

9) JESSE RYDER
Wellington v Otago, Wellington, 2013

To quote Ronan Keating, as Jesse Ryder is probably apt to do, life is a roller-coaster. In March 2013 he was the victim of an assault that left him in a medically induced coma, having suffered a fractured skull and a collapsed lung. Thankfully, he was OK and soon discharged from hospital, but in August of the same year it was announced that Ryder had tested positive for a banned substance in a routine drug test back in March, resulting in a six-month ban (which was backdated). Ryder made his return in October, having endured seven months out of the game. The opponents? His former team Wellington. The result? A century (117) for Ryder with 22 fours.

8) GEOFF BOYCOTT
England v Australia, Trent Bridge, 1977

So allegedly miffed was Boycott at being overlooked for the captaincy, that he went into a self-imposed England exile for three years between 1974 and 1977, missing out on 31 Test matches. But with the Aussies in town again in '77 he was back in the mix. Cue the deep nadir employed by the comeback-penning scriptwriters as he ran out Nottinghamshire local hero and hooking demi-god Derek Randall. His glove went to his face – it was his error and he looked genuinely sorry. But, never fear, he went on to score a century. It gets even better though – he was on 80 not out at the non-striker's end in the second dig as Randall hit the winning runs.

7) JOHN TRAICOS
Zimbabwe v India, Harare, 1992

Surrounded by superstars who lost complete Test careers when South Africa was exiled from the cricketing world, Egypt-born John Traicos went below the radar. He may have lacked the sumptuousness of Procter, Richards or Pollock, but he had one quality their international careers lacked: longevity. While politics and sport reached laboured agreement for South Africa's return, Traicos just carried on bowling orderly, thrifty off-spin. Having played in South Africa's last Test in 1970, he was well preserved enough to play in Zimbabwe's first in 1992. That gap of 22 years remains a beacon of hope for Test discards everywhere.

6) JEFF WILSON
New Zealand v Australia, Auckland, 2005

Here's proof that there is no intelligent designer responsible for our world. No single being – omnipotent or not – would be so cruel as to afford one man the ability to represent their country at two sports while rendering the majority of us unable to negotiate a walk in the park. Jeff Wilson was at one stage 11th on the list of all-time try scorers in international rugby union, and he ain't bad at cricket either. He made his New Zealand ODI debut in 1993, nipped off to become an All Black legend, and then made a cricketing comeback 12 years later in a T20 international. Nice work if you can get it.

5) WILFRED RHODES
England v Australia, The Oval, 1926

England selector Sir Pelham Warner managed to convince fellow selector Wilfred Rhodes that even at 48 he was still one of England's best spin options. "We think, Wilfred, that you should play: you are still the best slow left-handed bowler in England. You can still spin 'em, you know." And spin 'em he could. After four drawn Tests, Rhodes helped win the finale, and thus the urn, with his figures of 2 for 35 in the first innings and 4 for 44 in the second. Rhodes' story is why every single England selector since has always taken their boots to a match, just in case.

4) GRAHAM THORPE
England v South Africa, The Oval, 2003

The situation facing Graham Thorpe as he walked out to bat for England for the first time in 14 months was far from ideal – a much-discussed divorce behind him, an England career to reignite and his side 400 runs behind South Africa. England needed to win to draw the series and the left-hander had forced his way back into the side. The pressure was on. He scratched his way to 28 overnight – surviving a huge lbw call on nought – then came back the next day to put on a record-breaking 268 with Marcus Trescothick, making a thrilling comeback 124. England topped 600, took a lead and then Harmison and Bicknell – the latter enjoying a comeback series of his own – took over, duffing up and befuddling the South Africans in equal measure to give England the most unlikely of victories. Alec Stewart bowed out but Thorpe was back. One of the great games.

3) DENNIS AMISS
England v West Indies, The Oval, 1976

Seemingly terrorised by the demonic pace of Lillee and Thomson the previous summer, the usually solid Warwickshire opener hadn't played for England for over a year as West Indies (themselves possessing a half-handy battery of quicks) arrived for the final Test of the "grovel" series at The Oval in '76. Reinstated at the top of the order – and boasting a new back-and-across technique that would subsequently become the vogue method for dealing with pace – Amiss hit a courageous 203 against an attack comprising Andy Roberts, Vanburn Holder, Wayne Daniel and an on-form Michael Holding, who took 14 for 149 in the match as Clive Lloyd's men romped to a highly charged 3-0 drubbing.

2) EDDIE PAYNTER
Australia v England, Brisbane, 1933

After day two Eddie Paynter felt particularly unwell. He headed to hospital and was diagnosed with tonsillitis – time for some bed rest. England started their reply to Australia's 360 well but then suffered a collapse. At 216 for 6 it was a case of cometh the hour, cometh the bed-ridden man. Bedecked in a sun hat and fuelled by a meal of eggs, brandy and champagne, he wandered out to the crease, having checked himself out of hospital against the judgment of his nurses. Twenty-four runs later he was back in bed, still not out and still not well. He returned the next day, all upper lip and heroism, and fought his way to 83, winning even the Australian fans over with his belligerence. England went on to win the Test, and the Ashes, with Paynter sealing it with a six. "It were nowt but a sore throat," was the Lancastrian's assessment. Not too many believed that, though, and he even got a congratulatory mention in the House of Commons.

1) IAN BOTHAM
England v New Zealand, The Oval, 1986

"I don't live by 'the rules', you know. And if there's one other person who's influenced me in the way I think, someone who is a maverick, someone who does that to the system, then it's Ian Botham." The words of David Brent – ridiculous, of course, but oddly true when it comes to Botham's Test comeback in 1986. Dropped for two months after getting done for smoking cannabis, Botham returned to the England scene in a blaze of free-spirited glory. His first delivery saw Bruce Edgar edge behind, and left him level with Dennis Lillee as the leading Test wicket-taker. Shortly after, he trapped Jeff Crowe lbw to overtake Lillee and break the record. "Here's what I think of your selection policy... sure I've smoked the odd dooby, but will you piss off and leave me alone?" continues Brent. Doubt Beefy could have put it better himself. ■

Fee-fi-fo-fum: Curtly
Ambrose and
Courtney Walsh
loved nothing
better than gobbling
up batsmen

Bowling Partnerships

TOTEMS IN TANDEM

10) RAMADHIN AND VALENTINE
29 Tests in tandem: 224 wickets

One would struggle to find two more unlikely looking sporting heroes than these West Indies spinners. Alf Valentine, bespectacled and bookish, was a left-arm twirler; while Sonny Ramadhin, mousy and mustachioed, was a mystery spinner who delivered a potent cocktail of off-breaks and leggies. Such was their success during the West Indies tour of England in 1950 – in which they took 59 wickets between them – "those two little pals of mine" were immortalised by calypso legend Lord Kitchener.

9) AMBROSE AND WALSH
95 Tests in tandem: 762 wickets

Curtly Ambrose's mother used to ring a bell outside her Antiguan home every time her son took a wicket, so she was often rushed off her feet during a stellar career in which he claimed 630 victims in international cricket. His new-ball partner was somewhat ungainly, but Courtney Walsh sustained his threat and impeccable line and length over a 17-year international career. Of pacemen, only Glenn McGrath has more Test scalps than Walsh's 519. A former captain of Gloucestershire, the Jamaican was revered during his 11 seasons in the West Country and acquired a reputation for kindness rather unfashionable for a quick bowler.

8) LARWOOD AND VOCE
Four Tests in tandem: 41 wickets

These two former Nottinghamshire miners left the pit to become loyal and determined lieutenants to Douglas Jardine and were instrumental in the England captain's leg-theory plans for the Bodyline series of 1932/33. Left-armer Bill Voce was originally a slow bowler, and varied his pace with great effect throughout his career; while newsreel footage of Harold Larwood showed him to have a beautifully smooth run-up and delivery, and lightning pace. Unlike his bowling partner, Voce continued playing Test cricket after the Bodyline fall-out but was reluctant to discuss his infamy right until his death in 1984. Ostracised in his home country, Larwood moved to Australia, arriving on the same boat that had delivered him to the most controversial series of all time, and lived in Sydney until his death at the age of 90 in 1995.

7) LAKER AND LOCK
24 Tests in tandem: 206 wickets

Tony Lock bowled an angry spell of 1 for 37 against Australia at Old Trafford in 1956 when his Surrey spin twin conceded the same number of runs but took nine wickets, followed by a perfect ten in the second innings. And so it was: the quieter, erudite off-spinner Jim Laker headlined, while Lock delivered slow left-arm with the snarl of a fast bowler. Under the captaincy of Stuart Surridge, the duo helped Surrey win seven successive County Championships in the 1950s. Lock was also a useful batsman, but his career was a little overshadowed by a suspect quicker ball; while Laker's delivery from the commentary box was similarly unflappable to the manner in which he casually slung his sweater over his shoulder and strolled off the field having taken the best match-figures in first-class history.

6) LINDWALL AND MILLER
50 Tests in tandem: 345 wickets

They complemented each other beautifully: Keith Miller – charismatic, eccentric, explosive – and the less obtrusive Ray Lindwall with the classical action of a thoroughbred. The Aussie duo terrorised Test batsmen for a decade and were part of Bradman's 1948 "Invincibles" team. Lindwall was the quiet all-round champion sportsman who retired to run a florist, while mop-haired Miller, a former Aussie Rules player and Royal Australian Air Force pilot, would never have considered a life so sedate.

5) STATHAM AND TRUEMAN
35 Tests in tandem: 284 wickets

Like many double-acts, these two had very different styles and contrasting characters. The belligerent Fred Trueman took the game by the scruff of the neck and retired as England's leading wicket-taker. "Some men may have bowled faster than Trueman, but none has done so with more gusto," wrote Geoffrey Moorhouse. While the Yorkshire half of this duo generally hogged the limelight, his Red Rose partner Brian Statham, known as "George", went quietly about the business of taking 252 Test wickets and was one of the most well-liked cricketers of his generation. He still holds legendary status in his home county of Lancashire, for whom he took 1,816 wickets at an extraordinary average of 15.12.

4) HALL AND GRIFFITH
23 Tests in tandem: 157 wickets

Shirt flapping and tearing in from an enormous run, Wes Hall bowled two of the most famous last overs in Test history: in the tied Test at Brisbane in 1960, and at Lord's three years later when Colin Cowdrey batted out a draw with a broken arm. His silky smoothness was never quite matched by fellow Barbadian Charlie Griffith, whose main weapon was a lethal shorter ball – almost literally in the case of the Indian batsman Nari Contractor who suffered a life-threatening fractured skull after feeling its full force. Griffith's action was the subject of continuing controversy and he finished his career with 94 Test wickets, while Hall bagged almost twice as many before becoming a church leader and politician.

3) LILLEE AND THOMSON
26 Tests in tandem: 217 wickets

Dennis Lillee and Jeff Thomson were the unruly combination that petrified England during the Ashes series of 1974/75, sharing the new ball and an appetite for controversy. Lillee's action made the purists purr and was only temporarily inconvenienced by a serious back problem after taking 31 England wickets in 1972. Named in Australia's Test Team of the Century, he was an enduring entertainer, while Thomson, his partner-in-crime with the slingy action, didn't quite have the longevity or pedigree but can lay claim – and frequently does on the after-dinner circuit – to being the fastest bowler the game has ever seen.

2) WASIM AND WAQAR
61 Tests in tandem: 559 wickets

This duo were charismatic, handsome and the most potent pace-bowling combination produced on the subcontinent. Floppy-haired southpaw Wasim Akram used guile, variation and raw pace – Lara and Kallis both rate him as the best they faced – while Waqar Younis broke many a toe with his devastating yorkers and was an early practitioner of reverse-swing. Waqar and Sachin Tendulkar shared a Test debut at Karachi in 1989 and the Pakistani quick took the honours by bowling "The Little Master" for 15. Spells with Surrey and Glamorgan followed, while Wasim became a Lancashire legend after helping the county to a host of one-day trophies. Pakistan were always a fearsome prospect with these two in harness, none more so than on the 1992 tour of England when the pair shared 43 wickets to bowl their country to a famous series win.

1) WARNE AND MCGRATH
104 Tests in tandem: 1,001 wickets

The only spin/speed combination in our list takes top spot by sheer weight of statistics. Glenn McGrath's unerring accuracy and steep bounce throttled one end while Shane Warne delivered his full repertoire at the other. Both had a distinct dislike of batsmen, as several run-ins with officialdom would testify. The willowy McGrath became the first Australian fast bowler to 100 Tests, and the efficient economy of his high action was perhaps the secret of his longevity. While McGrath's title of the most prolific pace-bowling wicket-taker in Tests looks safe for the time being, Warne's overall record haul of 708 wickets will perhaps never be overtaken. "Love him or hate him," said Sri Lankan Kumar Sangakkara, "we were definitely very lucky to have him." ∎

Richie
and his
aphne

Cricketing Love Affairs

IT'S THE WHOLE 22 YARDS FOR THESE
STAR-CROSS'D LOVERS

10) KEITH MILLER AND PRINCESS MARGARET

An Ashes power couple for the ages. He was a dashing Australian
World War II fighter pilot turned all-conquering all-rounder. She
was the younger daughter of King George VI and younger sibling to
the eventual Queen of England, Elizabeth II. Women loved Miller,
and he had a lot of time for them too, but his relationship with
Margaret was built on more than just physical attraction. From
1948 onwards, whenever Miller was in England, the princess would
seek out his company. When asked about their association later in
life, Miller remarked, "Put it this way, we had a lot of fun."

9) BILL LAWRY AND TONY GREIG

"You're the Australian captain that lost 4-0 in South Africa, aren't you?"
"Yeah, and you're the guy who gave up the captaincy of England for money."

From the moment they met in the Channel 9 commentary box, just
two years after Greig had captained the World XI in World Series
Cricket, it was clear they were meant to be. A rapport that subsisted
on niggles but flourished with the utmost respect for one another,

Greig and Lawry were an iconic part of the Australian summer for more than 30 years. They would arrive at the ground together in Greig's car and dine with each other most nights. After Greig lost his battle with lung cancer in 2012, Lawry was understandably distraught. "I guess you could say I'm a bit lonely," he said. "A bit lost."

8) MITCHELL STARC AND ALYSSA HEALY

Starc and Healy – the niece of former Australian wicketkeeper Ian – first set eyes on each other when they were nine years of age and trialling to play representative cricket for the Northern District Cricket Association in Sydney. Both wicketkeepers, they shared duties behind the stumps before Starc started bowling more and Healy, at 15, began playing women's cricket. After losing contact for a few years, they rekindled a friendship that blossomed into something more and they tied the knot in 2016. The pair aren't all love and hugs, though. They've been banned from training together at their local indoor cricket centre, run by a friend, after, according to Starc, "it got a bit dangerous."

7) GRAEME SWANN AND JAMES ANDERSON

With the sort of buddy-comedy shtick that would make Paul Rudd blush, this bromance become one of the hallmarks of the England team which briefly reached No.1 in the ICC Test rankings in 2011. It's a relationship that seemed to flourish as much on the field as it did off it, with the duo helping each other take wickets on 31 occasions in Tests. They have also entertained on the airwaves as part of Greg James' *Not Just Cricket* series on BBC Radio 5 Live and shared the sofa on *Cricket AM*.

6) KEVIN PIETERSEN AND PIERS MORGAN

It's hard to pinpoint exactly when this union formed. What is clear is that, for all their Twitter jousting, no one outside of Kevin Pietersen's closed circle of confidants supports him more than Piers

Morgan. Certainly, no one fights the former England batsman's battles on his behalf so publicly. It was Morgan who got involved in the revealing of the identity of the scamp behind the infamous "KP Genius" parody Twitter account, before calling out the ECB and Andy Flower when Pietersen was dropped after sending BBM messages to opposing South African players during the summer of 2012. There's no denying the two have found a mutual appreciation of one another.

5) PIPPA MIDDLETON AND ALEX LOUDON

Alex Loudon was best known for possessing a legal doosra – a rarity for any bowler, let alone one cultivated outside of the subcontinent. But after retiring in 2007, turning down a two-year contract extension with Warwickshire to focus on a business career, the one-time England ODI all-rounder was out of sight and out of mind. That is, until Pippa Middleton came into our social conscience by virtue of being related to someone who got married to someone really famous. The pair split at the end of 2011, with Loudon reportedly growing weary of the media circus surrounding their relationship.

4) SHANE WARNE AND LIZ HURLEY

The finest leg-spinner the world has ever seen, and England's rose (sort of). Warne's courting of Hurley was there for all to see as they exchanged flirty tweets for months before it became clear this was something more significant. Both sought solace, and found it, after the end of their respective relationships – Warne with ex-wife Simone Callahan, Liz with husband of four years, Arun Nayar. The relationship remained firmly in public view, with 140-character kisses flying back and forth between the two, and confirmation followed in September 2011 that they were engaged. They went their separate ways in 2013, with Warne citing their busy schedules as the reason for the break-up, but they remain friends.

3) SHOAIB MALIK AND SANIA MIRZA

That Pakistan's then-captain was marrying India's No.1-ranked tennis player is the least outrageous part of a story that gripped both nations in 2010. Just days after the pair announced their marriage plans, a woman by the name of Ayesha Siddiqui alleged that she had married Malik in 2002 through a telephone nikah – an Islamic ceremony – something Malik had refuted in January 2008. There was also talk of deception, with Malik claiming the woman he thought he was entering into a relationship with in 2002 was not who she claimed to be in photos she had sent him. In the end, just days after denying he knew who Ayesha was, Malik granted her a divorce and married his beloved Mirza in Hyderabad.

2) BEEFY AND KATH

It was 26 June 1974, after a washed-out B&H Cup contest between Leicestershire and Somerset had afforded players, families and friends some extra time at the bar. Drowning in the clubhouse stench of smoke and stale booze, Kathryn Waller – a family friend of Brian Close, then Somerset captain – turned to the young man to her left and enquired as to whether he had got to watch any of the action that preceded the rain. The response from the 18-year-old was short: "Actually, I've been playing!" From then on, they were head over heels, as Botham embarked on his sometimes rocky road to legendary status and Kath settled into a life *Living With A Legend* – the title of her book released in 1987. Botham's big autobiography – *Don't Tell Kath...* – arrived seven years later and today, notwithstanding the odd historical tabloid splash, the first couple of English cricket remain very much together.

1) RICHIE AND DAPHNE BENAUD

The head of state and first lady of commentary, the Benauds were cricket's most revered couple before Richie's death in 2015. They met on a BBC television course, with Richie planning for a life beyond unblemished captaincy, and Daphne looking to make strides in an industry not especially open to women. She worked as a personal assistant for a number of cricket writers, including EW Swanton and, in 1961, she became the first woman allowed into a press box at a Test match. They married in 1967 and shared a love of cricket, fine wine and even *Harry Potter*, often reading the books in tandem. When Richie was involved in a minor car accident in 2013, Daphne was right behind her man. "Richie's remarkable," she said. "At first I was quite concerned but today he's looking unbelievably well." Even after six decades, they were still flirting. ■

Bhagwath Chandrasekhar believed his withered arm benefited his bowling

Soldiers

'TWAS NOTHING BUT A SCRATCH

10) MANOU'S TICKER

It is a mark of the Aussie cricketer's immense ticker that he could play a decade at the top despite having a hole in his. Graham Manou, the keeper who played an Ashes Test in 2009 when Brad Haddin went down injured, first found out he had a hole in his heart after experiencing chest pains as an 11-year-old, but battled against his condition to forge an excellent career in Australian domestic cricket. The erstwhile South Australia skipper organised a 960-mile "Tour de Heart" bike race in 2007 and 2008 to raise money for cardiac research.

9) GOUGHIE'S WHEEZING

Darren Gough's spirit would have seen off ebola, let alone respiratory issues, and it's that attitude that sustained him through a career in which his asthmatic problems were soundly thrashed. The condition was first diagnosed when he was a 19-year-old on Yorkshire's staff but, with the help of morning and evening doses of Ventolin, Gough was able to get through his career with only sporadic asthma attacks on the pitch.

8) WASIM'S DIABETES

In 1997 Wasim Akram's dad decided enough was enough. In the middle of Pakistan's Test series against West Indies, Akram senior dragged his boy to the quacks to get him checked out. The bowler, then 31, had lost a lot of weight and was constantly thirsty and tired. When diabetes was eventually diagnosed, Wasim was devastated but radical changes in his diet and training techniques, plus three injections of insulin every day, enabled him to keep playing for another six years.

7) ROWE'S SINUSES

Jamaica's rogue stylist made a hundred and a double on his Test debut, but that was as good as it got for Lawrence Rowe. A season with Derbyshire in 1974 was blighted by headaches and hayfever, and the problems persisted that winter in India, when he was sent home from the West Indies tour after further problems with his eyesight. Two years later the problems kicked off again in England, before he was finally diagnosed as suffering from a severe grass allergy. More remedial work on his eyes further affected his sight, and after struggling through a decade of infrequent brilliance, he finished up in 1983, by then a frustrated figure unwisely leading a West Indies rebel tour to South Africa.

6) CHANDRASEKHAR'S POLIO

A brilliant leggie from India's era of floppy hats and mesmerising tweakers, Bhagwath Chandrasekhar took 242 Test wickets in 58 Tests with his magic box of vicious toppers and googlies, all delivered at almost medium-pace from an arm withered by a brutal polio attack as a child. Chandra believes that his damaged arm actually helped him impart extra spin on the ball, though a "modest" batting average of 4 suggests the benefits to his cricket may have stopped there.

5) BOYCOTT'S EYESIGHT

Growing up in Yorkshire, Geoffrey Boycott was obsessed with making it as a pro cricketer, but it was a difficult slog to achieve. His first setback occurred when he ruptured his spleen, spending the next few years in and out of hospital. But his world really came crashing down when he was told as a 14-year-old that he required glasses. He initially thought his chance had gone, and so did many people involved in Yorkshire cricket. But Boycott wasn't having it. Aided by a pair of NHS glasses, the bespectacled Boycs set about adapting his game, and found he was able to still score big runs. Later in his career he switched to contact lenses and was written off again after a barren season. But he adjusted again, his eyes serving him well enough to make his 151st and final first-class hundred in 1986, aged 46.

4) GARRY'S EXTRA DIGITS

Sir Garfield Sobers must have known he was destined for greatness. How else to explain his decision as a child to personally remove the two extra fingers he was born with – one on each hand – with catgut and a sharp knife? Cutting off a couple of your own digits probably puts the courage needed to face fast bowling into perspective.

3) GREIG'S EPILEPSY

Tony Greig was first diagnosed with epilepsy after collapsing during a tennis match when he was 14, but for much of his professional career he hid his condition from his peers, even passing off a seizure during his Eastern Province debut in 1971 as heatstroke. But his illness was revealed when he suffered another fit at Heathrow Airport after returning from an Ashes tour in 1975, and the press soon began sniping about whether Greig's "problem" was affecting his decision-making capabilities as a captain. Four years later Greig left England for good, and he went on to campaign for greater awareness of the condition.

2) SIR LEN'S WITHERED ARM

Len Hutton was one of the very best around when World War II hit. But in a devastating moment during commando training he injured his left arm so badly that he was forced into hospital for eight months, eventually emerging – following three bone grafts – to a future in cricket with one arm two inches shorter than the other. But Hutton was a tough cookie, and after building up the strength in his arm with games in the Bradford League, he was eventually able to return. Some say he wasn't quite the same player, and it's true that the injury removed the hook and pull from his armoury, but Sir Len was still easily good enough to remain at the top of the world game for the next decade.

1) FRED'S LOST TOES

Fred Titmus, the wisecracking geezer from Kentish Town with magic in his fingers, was a no-nonsense sort of cricketer and one of the English game's greats. His career began in 1949 and finished 33 years later when the off-spinner popped into Lord's for a cuppa one morning and, after viewing a dry pitch from the dressing-room, was persuaded by Mike Brearley to don the whites one last time. Needless to say, the great man took three wickets in the second innings, Middlesex eventually took the title, and it brought the curtain down on a 2,830-wicket career. But it was almost a very different ending. On tour with England in 1967/68, Titmus was out swimming in the sea in Barbados when he suffered a horrific injury, getting his feet caught in the propeller of a boat and losing four toes in an accident that seriously threatened his career. It would have finished a lesser man's career, but Titmus was back for Middlesex the following summer, twirling again for the cause from a remodelled approach to the wicket, every hobbled delivery adding to the legend of the guvnor of NW8. ■

The
Bad

> **"CRICKET IS BASICALLY BASEBALL ON VALIUM"**
> ROBIN WILLIAMS

Squint really hard, and even cricket's filthiest bits can appear bathed in shimmering splendour. There's nothing so pointless, so triflingly naff or broadly rubbish in cricket that can't, with just a little effort, be infused with a sturdy magnificence. And so, let us turn to this: a compendium of irresistibly crap batsmen, thrillingly awful fielders, legendary noughts, run-outs on 99, the hoariest pretenders to Botham's crown, the most ill-judged gongs ever awarded and the very worst county seasons in history – not to mention the very worst overs – all tied around the most bucolically "village" moments in cricket's long and storied history. Bursting with ineptitude, knee-deep in human frailty, dripping with the agonies, misfortunes and gnawing defeats for which cricket serves us all so well, it's all here. Dig in.

Village Moments

WHEN THE PROFESSIONAL GAME
PLUNGES TO AMATEUR LEVELS

10) WALKING ON AIR

Alan Mullally's bowling boots were shot to pieces after some hard yakka on the 1998/99 Ashes tour, leaving him no choice but to go shopping for a new pair. Eschewing more conventional cricket outlets, England's left-armer headed to the bright lights of NikeTown, picking himself up a pair of Air Jordan 14 basketball pumps. They looked truly awful but did the business, as Mullally took out Australia's top four at Brisbane to finish with ODI-best figures of 4 for 18 and scoop the Man of the Match award. "The best boots I ever wore in my life," he later said.

9) EVERY DOG HAS ITS DAY

What is it about Jack Russells and Test matches at the Wanderers? Almost 20 years to the day since the hirsute Gloucestershire stumper dug himself a hole and spent four hours in it to halt South Africa's victory charge, another pesky terrier put a spanner in the works as the Proteas prepared for the Joburg Test in January 2016. Quinton de Kock had been taking an afternoon stroll with his two Jack Russells when he slipped and twisted his right knee, forcing South Africa to send for Dane Vilas on the morning of the match. Efforts were made to spare the keeper's blushes by keeping schtum about the circumstances surrounding his injury but thankfully teammate Dean Elgar decided the story was too good not to share and spilled the beans.

8) WHAT'S UP, DOC?

England's squad were dropping like flies on the 1994/95 Ashes tour, with six replacements called up in all. Things went from bad to worse when team physio Dave Roberts was thrown in as an emergency sub-fielder for a tour match at Bendigo and proceeded to break his finger in the warm-up, leaving England a man down and their medical practitioner on the treatment table.

7) ASHES BURN

England's 2013/14 Ashes tour had already reached humiliating levels of rubbishness by the time the series reached Perth but the omnishambles that led to the run-out of Shane Watson did at least provide some light relief. Pushing for a declaration, Watto heaved Tim Bresnan high into the sky, Ian Bell steadied himself to take a dolly and promptly dropped it. Bresnan, furious, hurled the ball at the stumps and obliterated them, with Watson – who hadn't bothered running – well short of his ground. Bell walked off distraught at shelling the chance, oblivious to the fact that Watson was on his way back to the pavilion.

6) HALES FAIL

"I'm quite forgetful," Alex Hales said in January 2016. "I'm the sort of guy who'll forget to pay a room bill in a hotel, or leave a passport behind. Important stuff." Two weeks later and Sloppy Al, as he's known to his teammates, walked out to bat in a T20 international at Newlands with the back of his England shirt covered in white tape. It later emerged that he'd been tardy putting his kit in the wash and had been forced to borrow Chris Woakes' shirt while his dried. Proper village.

5) LAYING DOWN THE GAUNTLETS

It's a sorry state of affairs when a keeper unstraps the pads and trundles in for a bowl in a club match, let alone a Test match, and even more so when said stumper is the King of Cool, MS Dhoni. There was something oddly unbecoming about India's slick skipper reducing himself to a military medium-pacer during the Lord's Test of 2011 after an injury took Zaheer Khan out of the attack. He did a decent job, though, nearly dismissing Kevin Pietersen, only for a caught-behind dismissal to be overturned on review.

4) A KEEP OF FAITH

It's even worse when the person who's not sure what they're doing is the wicketkeeper. It's such a specialist position, but we probably take their skills for granted. When they get injured, a hush descends on the field. What on earth happens now? What follows is a professional sportsman, skilled in the art of catching, putting on gloves and looking like he's never before noticed he had arms, let alone used the hands on the end of those arms to catch. The gloves are all flappy, the pads aren't right, he's not even competent at offloading the ball to first slip. England have previous, the best example being Anthony McGrath filling in for Alec Stewart in 2003 and looking like someone's grumpy stepbrother who had been persuaded to turn out for the third XI.

3) IN THE BLACK

As if a Texan fraudster with wandering hands and £5bn worth of ill-gotten gains hosting the England cricket team for a $20m dollar winner-takes-all match wasn't rank enough, the Stanford Super Series plunged new depths with its truly criminal approach to aesthetics. Allen Stanford's trademark black bats, which all players were forced to use, made the sorry circus look like a souped-up game of Kwik Cricket.

2) RUB OF THE BAGGY GREEN

When Mitchell Starc busted his foot during the 2015 Adelaide Test against New Zealand, Aussie skipper Steve Smith took the curious decision to send out the team masseur as twelfth man rather than calling for one of the allocated sub-fielders. A former Victoria second-XI cricketer and one-time Aussie Rules draftee, Grant Baldwin looked built for the task, but after couple of fumbles Smith thought better of it and opted to call up a pro in his place.

1) "COME QUICK, BRAD CAN'T GET HIS TROUSERS ON"

A talented batsman with a colourful rap sheet, Luke Pomersbach's career was heading southward after a boozy session with Shaun Marsh led to the pair being banned by Western Australia. At a loose end, he decided to kick back with his girlfriend at a T20 international against New Zealand, only to receive an 11th-hour summons to the Aussie dressing-room when Brad Hodge crocked his back putting his trousers on. Batting at No.6, Pomersbach slammed his second ball over the ropes in a seven-ball cameo worth 15 in what would prove to be his only international appearance. ■

The Stanford Super Series was an unmitigated disaster, and the black bats didn't help

Wayne Larkins
on the drive

Unfortunate England Careers

ENGLAND INTERNATIONALS WHOSE TIME AT THE
TOP WAS NOT WHAT IT SHOULD HAVE BEEN

10) WAYNE LARKINS

13 Tests: 493 runs at 20.54
25 ODIs: 591 runs at 24.62

Blessed with enough natural talent for two batsmen, Wayne "Ned" Larkins was a cavalier opener who never quite translated his flair to the international stage. Larkins did himself no favours by joining the 1982 rebel tour of South Africa – and the resultant ban deprived England of much of his cricketing prime – but he was also unlucky that all but two of his 13 Test matches were against the powerhouses of his day, West Indies and Australia. Who knows what he could have achieved given proper backing, although question marks persisted over his temperament. "He was an intense admirer of Gordon Greenidge and had all his skill and panache but only a smidgen of his hunger," Simon Hughes once observed. "He was a simple man of simple pleasures. Offer him a bouncy wicket, a hearty lunch and a few beers, and he was happy."

9) ROBIN SMITH

62 Tests: 4,236 runs at 43.67
71 ODIs: 2,419 runs at 39.01

Robin Smith, or the Judge as he was known to his legions of admirers, was a batsman who relished the thrill of facing fast bowling and possessed a cut shot that sounded like a backfiring cannon. He was England's most assured batsman during the early Nineties, and his brutal unbeaten 167 against Australia in 1993 was the highest score by an Englishman in ODIs until Alex Hales broke his record in 2016. There is a school of thought that Smith was simply too nice for international cricket – his frank admission that he struggled against top-class spin bowling and his easy friendships with opposing players are often cited as examples. Yet the overwhelming impression is that when he was finally dropped (following England's 1995/96 tour of South Africa, despite an assured half-century in the final Test), England discarded a performer who still had plenty to give.

8) MARTYN MOXON

10 Tests: 455 runs at 28.43
8 ODIs: 174 runs at 21.75

It's always easy to blame the umpire for your misfortunes, but during England's 1987/88 tour of New Zealand the men in white well and truly stuffed Martyn Moxon. Having been denied three runs early in his innings when a middled sweep shot was mystifyingly signalled as leg-byes, Moxon, almost inevitably, found himself dismissed one short of his maiden Test century. The cruel hand of fate was not finished there. Moxon was 81 not out overnight going into the third day of the following match at Wellington, only for the heavens to open and the match to be rained off. After a summer being peppered by missiles dished out by the visiting West Indies quicks and enduring England's wretched '89 Ashes series, he was promptly dropped, never to return. He remains one of an exclusive group to have scored 99 in a Test career without ever making a century.

7) JAMES TAYLOR

7 Tests: 312 runs at 26
27 ODIs: 887 runs at 42.23

Churning out county runs in all forms since he was in short trousers (which, as it happens, he never grew out of), James Taylor had to wait a long time before being truly embraced by the England management. A brief stint in 2012 didn't impress Kevin Pietersen, and it wasn't until late 2015 that Taylor – one of the country's finest players of spin and a brilliant short-leg fielder – finally established himself as a regular in England's Test and one-day sides. But then in April 2016 disaster struck when, at the age of 26, he was diagnosed with an incurable heart condition and forced to retire immediately. Taylor finished his career with the third-highest List A average (53.11) of all time.

6) ANDY LLOYD

1 Test: 10 runs, not dismissed
3 ODIs: 101 runs at 33.66

There are few tougher introductions to international cricket than facing Malcolm Marshall on a flier, but that is the fate that befell Warwickshire opener Andy Lloyd. Selected to make his Test debut on his home ground of Edgbaston following some solid form in the preceding ODI series, Lloyd toughed it out for half an hour before a vicious bumper crashed into his helmet and landed him a full week in hospital. Lloyd did not play again that season and was never recalled by England, although he battled back to play 299 first-class games for Warwickshire, and thus possesses the unique record of being the only player to open a Test innings and never be dismissed.

5) MARTIN BICKNELL

4 Tests: 14 wickets at 38.78
7 ODIs: 13 wickets at 26.69

It's a sad world when 1,061 first-class wickets are insufficient to earn you more than four Test caps. Martin Bicknell was the bedrock upon which the all-conquering Surrey side of the early Noughties was built. Bicknell made his Test bow during the 1993 Ashes series, but injury wrecked his chances of making England's winter tour and from there on he was battling it out with Angus Fraser and Andy Caddick to share the new ball with Darren Gough. It was a battle that Bicknell, despite stacks of wickets and some 6,740 first-class runs, was destined to lose again and again.

He did eventually have his moment in the sun. Surprisingly recalled to the Test side to face South Africa in 2003 at the age of 34, he took a wicket with his first ball at Headingley and bowled England to a memorable, series-levelling victory in the next Test at The Oval. "It's without doubt my fondest memory of playing for England; it's the only Test match I played in that we actually won," said Bicknell. "To be on the winning side playing for England on your home pitch is going to stay with me for the rest of my life."

4) BILLY BATES
15 Tests: 50 wickets at 16.42

A tragic story. Billy Bates was a gifted, big-turning off-spinner and a good enough batsman to open for England, but his career was cut short during the 1887/88 Ashes tour when he was struck in the face by a cricket ball while bowling in the nets. The blow damaged his eyesight to such an extent that he was unable to continue his first-class career, an awful turn of events that drove him to attempt suicide. His sight eventually recovered enough for him to forge a second career as a coach in his native Yorkshire, but he was afforded little time in his new profession as he passed away at the age of 45.

3) HAROLD LARWOOD
21 Tests: 78 wickets at 28.35

Few bowlers throughout history earned themselves such an intimidating reputation as Harold Larwood. A previous life spent working in the coalmines of Nottinghamshire granted him formidable powers of strength and stamina, while his stature (he stood just 5ft 8in in his socks) meant that his lightning-quick bouncer homed in on the batsman's ribs and jaw. A hard, intensely loyal man, he was a captain's dream, prepared to bend his back on unresponsive pitches and bowl all day, so long as there was a beer and a cigarette to hand at the interval.

He was Douglas Jardine's weapon of choice during the infamous Bodyline tour, utilised relentlessly and instructed to bowl through a painful foot injury at the SCG because Don Bradman, the principal target behind the "leg theory" strategy, was still at the crease. The hostile, short-pitched barrage Larwood and Bill Voce – his partner-in-crime for Notts and England – subjected the Australians to was so potent that a diplomatic incident ensued. Larwood, simply by doing what he was told to do by his famously provocative captain, was rapidly made a scapegoat for the sake of the Empire. He never played for England again, a fate that tellingly did not befall Jardine.

Injuries gradually took their toll and Larwood retired from first-class cricket in 1938. He emigrated to Sydney in 1950 and, to his immense surprise, was welcomed with open arms by a nation who recognised a steely, honest competitor when they saw one. It's a shame the English hierarchy of the time could not do the same.

2) BUDDY OLDFIELD
I Test: 99 runs at 49.50

Many cricketers have played a solitary Test match for England, but none of them scored more runs than Buddy Oldfield. Called up to face West Indies at The Oval in August 1939, he shared a 131-run stand with Len Hutton on his way to making a composed 80 in first innings and added 19 further runs in the second innings as the match wound its way to a hard-fought draw. A few days later, World War II erupted. When it eventually finished, the 35-year-old Oldfield could not agree terms with his county, Lancashire, and retired to play league cricket, contenting himself with a record of 17,811 first-class runs, 38 centuries and one impressive Test appearance.

1) COLIN MILBURN
9 Tests: 654 runs at 46.71

Colin Milburn was 18 stone of unadulterated raconteur, adored by public and players alike. He could play a bit, too. An opening bat for England, Northants and Western Australia, he had a textbook defence and wonderful hands; it was said that if a bowler strayed to leg he might as well have kissed the ball goodbye such was Milburn's power. He was called up to the Test side in 1966 and took to the international game like a duck to water, making 94 in his first Test against the mighty West Indies and smashing an unbeaten 126 at Lord's. He was surprisingly dropped because of his less-than-spritely fielding for the final Test of the summer, but won his place back the following year and in his final international innings (during England's winter tour of Pakistan in 1969) he dismembered a talented attack to the tune of 139 runs.

Sadly, Milburn was involved in a serious car accident later that year which cost him his left eye and – despite his brave efforts to resume his career in 1973 and '74, a period where he made just one-half century – he was never the same player again. He was later struck down by a heart attack, aged just 48. ■

Notorious Drops

CATCHES WIN MATCHES BUT IT'S OFTEN
THE DROPS THAT LINGER THE LONGEST

10) FLINTOFF DROPS FLINTOFF
England v West Indies, Edgbaston, 2004

Such was Andrew Flintoff's supreme control during his career-best 167, he even found time to pick out his old man in the crowd with an almighty clump over mid-wicket. Unfortunately for Flintoff Snr, a stalwart of Whittingham and Goosnargh third XI, the chance was shelled and the family ribbing commenced: "I see my dad rise from his seat, big smile on his face, his nickname's 'Colin Big Hands', but in front of everyone he drops it. More embarrassing than that, trying to catch the rebound it spills out of his hands and into Michael Vaughan's mum's lap, so he's there, head buried between her legs. Not a good day for my dad, that."

9) MARK WAUGH'S LONDON BUS SYNDROME
Australia v Pakistan, Colombo, 2002

With 181 Test catches to his name, Mark Waugh is rightly considered to be one of the greatest slip snafflers of all time. So an air of utter disbelief descended on Colombo when Waugh dropped three sitters on the same day as Australia sought victory over Pakistan. The misses did not cost his team – Australia went on to win the match – but with reflexes waning it was a stark signal that time had finally caught up with "Junior" and he only wore the Baggy Green twice more before he called time on his illustrious Test career.

8) GRAHAM THORPE "DROPS THE ASHES"
England v Australia, Headingley, 1997

During the Nineties it was rare for an Ashes series to still be alive come the fourth Test, but in the 1997 series England and Australia were locked together at one apiece. Gloucestershire seamer and Test debutant Mike Smith was chucked the ball at a critical point with Australia rocking on 50 for 4 in reply to England's 172. In his second over Smith found the edge of Matthew Elliott's blade to offer the simplest of chances for Graham Thorpe at slip but somehow the Surrey man couldn't hold on. Elliott went on to make 199 and England lost by an innings. When Thorpe apologised to his skipper, Michael Atherton reportedly recycled Gubby Allen's line to Walter Robbins after the latter had dropped Bradman in 1936/37. "Don't worry Thorpey, you've only cost us the Ashes." Smith remained wicketless and was never picked again.

7) ASHLEY GILES DROPS THE PUNT
Australia v England, Adelaide, 2006

Duncan Fletcher's strong preference for multi-dimensional cricketers was no doubt central to Ashley Giles getting the nod over Monty Panesar at the start of the 2006/07 Ashes. So irony loomed large when Giles let slip a relatively simple chance at deep square leg that would have seen Ricky Ponting depart for 35 and reduce the Aussies to 78 for 4 in reply to England's 551 for 6 declared. Ponting cashed in to the tune of 145, helping Australia pass 500 before the Aussies skittled England on the final morning to set up the most unlikely – and sickening – of victories.

6) CHRIS SCOTT'S MOST EXPENSIVE DROP IN HISTORY
Warwickshire v Durham, Edgbaston, 1994

"I suppose he'll get a hundred now," Durham's journeyman keeper Chris Scott reportedly said after putting down a straightforward catch to remove Brian Lara for just 18. With Lara going into the match having recorded six tons in seven first-class innings, Scott's assumption was understandable. Unfortunately for Scott and Durham, his prediction proved to be only partially accurate, as Lara went on to plunder another 483 runs to record the highest-ever first-class score of 501 not out.

5) IAN HEALY AND THE MIRACLE OF BRIDGETOWN
West Indies v Australia, Bridgetown, 1999

Five years later, Ian Healy's drop of Lara may not have cost 483 runs (in fact the great man added only another six), but in many ways it was a more significant blunder. Few gave the Windies a hope at the start of day five, especially when 85 for 3 soon became 105 for 5 in search of 308. But Lara refused to conform to the script and ad-libbed his way to a breathtaking century. However, with seven runs needed and West Indies eight down, Australia's get-out-of-jail card appeared to have arrived when Lara guided one straight to Healy's left mitt. In his younger days Healy would have gone with two hands and taken the catch with ease but, aged 35, he could only palm the ball to the floor. The ninth wicket fell soon after but crucially Lara was still at the crease to hit the winning runs and secure a one-wicket victory.

4) HERSCHELLE GIBBS "DROPS THE WORLD CUP"
South Africa v Australia, Headingley, 1999

When Steve Waugh came to the crease in the final match of the Super Sixes (a contest the Aussies had to win to progress) his team were in a spot of bother in pursuit of South Africa's imposing 271. A Herschelle Gibbs ton provided the backbone of that innings and his day should have got even better when Waugh clipped the simplest of chances to him at mid-wicket. Gibbs gleefully accepted the present only to let the ball squirm from his grip as he attempted to hurl the ball skywards in celebration. Waugh later denied the famous quip which supposedly followed, but the sentiment if not the words were entirely accurate – he went on to make 120 from 110 balls, and Australia secured victory with two deliveries left before going on to lift the trophy.

3) GATT LOSES HIS BEARINGS
India v England, Chennai, 1993

While Mike Gatting's insatiable appetite may be legendary, one thing he inexplicably failed to gobble up during England's disastrous 1992/93 tour of India was perhaps the simplest chance in the history of Test cricket. When Ian Salisbury ripped one from the Chennai rough into the glove of Kiran More, the ball could not possibly have taken a slower, more gentle trajectory toward the welcoming hands of Gatting at silly point. Astonishingly, with umpire RS Rathore's finger already raised, Gatting conspired to reject the gift and the cherry came to rest in front of a giggling Graeme Hick at slip.

2) KIRAN MORE DROPS THE DADDY
England v India, Lord's, 1990

Graham Gooch was on just 36 when Sanjeev Sharma found his edge to provide the most regulation of caught-behind chances for Kiran More. "Oh... dear" was Richie Benaud's typically understated reaction to the Teflon-gloved spillage. Gooch went on to amass 333. More reflects: "I clearly remember it was a straightforward catch, except in England the ball wobbles a bit in the air after it passes the bat and that's a test for a keeper. I failed the test on that occasion."

1) SHANE WARNE GRASSES KP
England v Australia, The Oval, 2005

Having almost single-handedly kept Australia in the series with 40 wickets at 19.92 and 249 runs at 27.66, it was cruel of the London crowd to tuck into Shane Warne with quite such relish. That said, chants of "Warnie's dropped the Ashes" weren't too far off the money. England were wobbling, three down with a lead of just 95, when a pumped-up Brett Lee found Kevin Pietersen's outside edge. Warne hadn't dropped a thing all summer but on this day of days the simple chance was spurned. KP took full advantage, hitting Warne for a pair of sixes in the very next over en route to a maiden Test century that would set off a national knees-up. ∎

David Lawrence
looked destined
for stardom before
being struck down
by a horrific injury

Accursed Gongs

CRICKETERS WHO FOUND THAT AWARDS ARE NO GUARANTEE OF GREATNESS

10) DAN CULLEN
Bradman Young Cricketer of the Year Award, 2006

Life after Warne didn't always look so gloomy for Australian cricket. Soon after finishing his lap of honour during the 2006/07 Ashes, the great impresario nominated off-spinner Dan Cullen, Australia's Young Cricketer of the Year, as his ready-made replacement. The South Australian had already made his Test debut at Chittagong in 2006, and would go on to win five ODI caps, but soon after Warne's anointment his form fell away, and the wicket of Mashrafe Mortaza would remain the first and only highlight of his Test career. Subsequent disappointing domestic returns led to the withdrawal of Cullen's national contract and he retired in 2009 at the age of 25.

9) GARY PRATT
NBC Denis Compton Award, 1999 (Durham)

Most famous as the gun sub-fielder who provoked Ricky Ponting's sweary exit during the 2005 Trent Bridge Test, Gary Pratt was once considered more than just a brilliant extra-cover. Having risen through the ranks with Durham, he won the county's NBC Compton Award for the club's best young player in 1999, receiving specialist tutelage in South Africa alongside fellow starlets Ian Bell and Ryan

Sidebottom. By 2003, Pratt had established himself in Durham's first team, passing 1,000 runs for the season, but that was as good as it got. Two years after the Ponting run-out, Pratt was playing non-league football for Crook Town FC. Hurt by his release from Durham in 2006, he partly blamed it on the run-out, which he felt marked him unfairly as "just a fielder". Pratt went on to torment bowlers across the north-east, scoring prolifically for Bishop Auckland and Cumberland.

8) GREG WOOD
NBC Denis Compton Award, 2005 (Yorkshire)

Wood was a superb all-round talent as a teenager, and a stellar professional career seemed assured for the Yorkshire prodigy. He won the 2004 Bunbury Festival spin-bowling scholarship (despite being widely recognised as a keeper-batsman), captained England under-19s in 2007 aged 17, and was sent out to a South African finishing school alongside fellow 2005 NBC Compton Award winners Alastair Cook, Stuart Broad and Luke Wright. Despite this promise, Wood only managed a solitary outing for Yorkshire's first XI, making a run-a-ball 26 against Sri Lanka A in 2007. Frustrated by a lack of opportunities, he parted company with the Tykes at the end of the 2009 season and left the professional game after a spell on the books at Notts.

7) IRFAN PATHAN
ICC Emerging Player of the Year, 2004

Thrust into an international debut against Australia in 2003 at the age of 19, the Indian left-arm seamer appeared the natural heir to Zaheer Khan following a host of wickets and Man of the Match awards. Capping his first season with India by becoming the first man to take a hat-trick in the first over of a Test match, Pathan was the natural choice for the ICC's Emerging Player gong for 2004. Yet, as his embryonic batting career blossomed, his swingers mysteriously lost their nip. Pathan has since found a new home as a limited-overs specialist and has been a hit in the IPL, but his international career promised so much more.

6) DAVID LAWRENCE
Cricket Writers' Club Young Cricketer of the Year, 1985

A cult hero of the county scene during the 1980s, this West Country warrior offered pace and heart by the bucketful. Having become a firm favourite at Gloucestershire, Lawrence impressed with his early England performances. A list of victims including Richie Richardson, Desmond Haynes and Viv Richards gave a tantalising glimpse of his talent, before horrific injury struck. Screaming in to bowl at the fag-end of a dead Test in New Zealand, Lawrence suffered a shocking knee fracture; the pistol-crack sound of his shattering kneecap could be heard all around the empty stadium. He never played for England again. With typical spirit, Lawrence battled back to regain fitness and returned for Gloucestershire five years later, but he was forced to quit for good in 1997, unable to generate the pace that was previously his hallmark.

5) CHRIS GAYLE
ICC LG People's Choice, 2011

It's 2011, and the people have spoken... Drum roll, please... The WINNER of the ICC's "People's Ineffable Champion in the Category Sponsored by a Washing Machine Company" is... CHRIS GAYLE! Man of the people. LONG LIVE DEMOCRACY!

4) AJANTHA MENDIS
ICC Emerging Player of the Year, 2008

A right old hoopla accompanied the emergence of Sri Lanka's ex-army officer turned mini-Murali mystery man. And quite right too, because Ajantha Mendis' early brilliance suggested the great void in spin bowling left by the retirements of Warne, Kumble and Murali would at least be partially filled. But the wonderful oddness of his trademark carrom ball – which made mugs of batsmen during that first year – lost its magic. And while Mendis has continued to make appearances for Sri Lanka, his initial reputation as a potential great hasn't come to fruition.

3) SIMON JONES
Wisden Cricketer of the Year, 2006

What would Simon Jones have achieved if injury hadn't cut him short? It's one of the lingering questions carried over from an era when England had an answer for just about everything. He was the fragile thoroughbred of the 2005 Ashes, a natural match-winner who ripped through Australia that summer, reverse-swinging his name into the Ashes annals and bagging, along with Kevin Pietersen, a celebrity invite to London Fashion Week – proof of sorts that cricket was scrubbing up nice again. But with *Wisden*'s award safely bagged and the champagne still flowing, his body rebelled prematurely against that devastating whiplash action and just gave up on him. Despite numerous operations and stuttering comebacks with Worcestershire, Glamorgan and Hampshire, he never quite got back on the catwalk again.

2) MARK LATHWELL
Cricket Writers' Club Young Cricketer of the Year, 1993

Hailed by his Somerset coach Bob Cottam as "the best young player I've ever seen," Mark Lathwell's career was blighted by the weight of expectation. Following a free-flowing start to his career that moved a swooning *Wisden* to compare him to Gower in his pomp, the wristy opener was fast-tracked into England's 1993 Ashes team when Graham Gooch's sinking ship threw out the old guard and plumped for kids. Up against a rampant Australian side and with his early season form having deserted him, the shy, homespun 21-year-old was mercilessly bullied by Merv Hughes and dropped after just two Tests. Being voted Cricket Writers' Club Young Cricketer of the Year was some consolation, but in truth Lathwell was already on the slide.

He never graced the international stage again and retired in 2001, after too many seasons of disappointment, to become a postman.

In his autobiography, Marcus Trescothick lamented the circumstances that led to his former teammate quitting the game: "I cannot overstate how brilliant Lathwell was. Sure, he found the experience of playing for England unnerving. The rumour goes that when Graham Gooch rang him up to tell him he was being left out... he mumbled something along the lines of 'Thank God for that.' But what a talent – a little bit of genius... when he tried a comeback he realised his heart was no longer in it, which was a tragedy for him and for English cricket."

1) MOHAMMAD AMIR
ICC Emerging Player of the Year nominee, 2010

Mohammad Amir was a shoo-in for the ICC's hip young buck award in 2010. In a summer of terror for England's batsmen he had just become the youngest bowler ever to take 50 Test wickets. Then he overstepped gigantically at Lord's, the cricket world caved in and the ICC were forced into action. The nominees for the award had already been announced, with Amir one of the star turns. Now, with the spot-fixing scandal engulfing the game, the ICC figured he had to go. And so, three weeks before the big event, an ICC spokesman confirmed that Amir had in fact been expunged from the shortlist, adding darkly: "Amir's removal could be confirmed by 'reading between the lines'." Six months later the ICC's stance was vindicated when Amir and two other Pakistani players were found guilty of spot-fixing and he was banned for five years. In a more nuanced but no less meaningful statement, Wisden's "Five" Cricketers of the 2010 season were reduced to four, leaving a gaping hole where the outrageously talented Amir would otherwise have stood. He would make a return to Test cricket in 2016 at Lord's, the scene of his crime. ∎

Steve Harmison's opening delivery of the 2006/07 Ashes set the tone for what was to follow

Worst Overs

THOSE OCCASIONS WHERE IT ALL
WENT HORRIBLY WRONG

10) MICK LEWIS, SOUTH AFRICA V AUSTRALIA – JOHANNESBURG, MARCH 2006

Ambling up to defend 434, Australia's rotund seamer Mick Lewis would have felt fairly comfortable that however he bowled, victory was assured. But this was no ordinary match, and when Herschelle Gibbs carted Lewis' seventh over for 18, the mother of all run chases was on. The Victorian right-armer went on to concede 113 runs from ten wicketless overs – at the time of writing the most expensive figures in ODI history – and never wore the Baggy Green again.

9) STEVE HARMISON, AUSTRALIA V ENGLAND – BRISBANE, NOVEMBER 2006

One over in – one ball, even – and we already knew how the whole thing was going to go. It was just a question of whether you sat there with your hot Bovril and watched the nightmare unfold, or went to bed ready to be clobbered with all of it at once in the morning. Abject isn't the word – a prize horse had gone lame, and captain Andrew Flintoff had no sugar cubes to cheer him up. Flintoff's nonchalant snare at second slip after Steve Harmison sent the opening delivery of the series straight into his hands was an unforgettable image. Overs have gone for more runs, but few have so accurately predicted the tone of a contest.

8) CURTLY AMBROSE, AUSTRALIA V WEST INDIES – PERTH, FEBRUARY 1997

Utterly inexplicable. Perhaps he hadn't had his Weetabix, or maybe someone sabotaged his wristbands, but Curtly wasn't his usual self as he sent down nine front-foot no-balls. The 15-ball over, which couldn't have been much fun for batsmen Shane Warne and Andy Bichel as they were all on target, ended up taking 12 minutes. Seeing one of the world's greatest fail repeatedly at such a rudimentary skill just felt a bit wrong, like Caravaggio gone colour-blind.

7) SCOTT BOSWELL, LEICESTERSHIRE V SOMERSET – LORD'S, SEPTEMBER 2001

Every so often, somewhere in the Midlands a man named Scott Boswell wakes up terrified in the middle of the night with visions of Marcus Trescothick's benign smile and umpire George Sharp's arms spread wide. It was the biggest game of his short-lived career. A Lord's final, no less. Given the new ball, Boswell got swallowed up by the yips, sending down eight wides in his second over, sweat and nerves making merry hell with his preparation. They swerved down the leg side, they wobbled down the off side, they eluded the cut strip for five deliveries in a row. It was all too embarrassing for words, apart from the crimson-faced, scrumpy-pickled men in the bleachers, whose happy chants of "Somerset! La-la-la!" still haunt Boswell's nightmares to this day.

6) RP SINGH, ENGLAND V INDIA – THE OVAL, AUGUST 2011

Ian Botham called it spot on when he termed this the worst first over of a Test match he'd ever seen. It really was that bad. A replacement for the injured Zaheer Khan in the same way as Paul Rodgers was a replacement for Freddie Mercury, Singh seemed a fraction of a fast bowler on this morning at The Oval. He gently floated five out of six balls down the leg side with a bored, trancelike lack of intensity only partially explained by the fact he hadn't bowled a first-class delivery in anger for seven months.

5) GLADSTONE SMALL, WARWICKSHIRE V MIDDLESEX –
COVENTRY, AUGUST 1982

As a 21-year-old Bajan trying to make an impression on his prospective new employers, the young Gladstone Small mislaid the plot. After sending down ten no-balls, he shortened his run-up to two paces, but the concentration of stepping behind the line and keeping it on the pitch at the same time was too much and he bowled a wide. In response his captain, Dennis Amiss, reportedly said, "When I said give us three or four quick overs at the start, I didn't mean all at once."

4) MARK BOUCHER, WEST INDIES V SOUTH AFRICA –
ANTIGUA, APRIL 2005

Some things just aren't right. While this over actually netted a wicket, the sight of a wicketkeeper-batsman of Mark Boucher's calibre debasing himself with a novelty turn as a bowler wasn't a great advert for Test cricket. Faced with West Indies' soporific, creaking 700-plus total, Graeme Smith thought there was no option left but to bowl every one of his 11 players as the match descended into farce. The episode proved especially embarrassing for Dwayne Bravo, who somehow ended up being dismissed by the South African stumper.

3) MOHAMMAD SAMI, BANGLADESH V PAKISTAN –
COLOMBO, JULY 2004

This over, during an Asia Cup tie, is the longest ever bowled in an ODI. Sami took 17 balls to finish it, and who can blame him? Faced with the sight of batting titans Habibul Bashar and Rajin Saleh – with a combined career average approaching that of a half decent No.8 – whose legs wouldn't turn to jelly? Sami eventually pulled himself together and finished the over but not before getting his name in the record books when he really rather wished he hadn't.

2) BERT VANCE, WELLINGTON V CANTERBURY – CHRISTCHURCH, FEBRUARY 1990

Wellington needed to win their final game of the season to ensure they took home the Shell Trophy. It looked unlikely with two wickets required in two overs, and Canterbury's penultimate pair Lee Germon and Roger Ford content to block, 95 runs from victory. So coach and captain put their heads together and came up with a cunning plan to dangle the carrot. Instructions were passed to part-timer Bert Vance, who bowled no-ball after no-ball as the batsmen pasted him to and over the boundary past motionless fielders. A grand total of 77 runs came off the over. But the farce didn't end there. The scorers had understandably failed to keep up, and no one knew how many were required from the last, meaning that Germon, having taken 17 off the first five balls, blocked the last with just one required for victory. It turned out Wellington needn't have bothered, as results elsewhere, and a sympathetic decision not to deduct points, meant they won the title anyway.

1) BEN STOKES, ENGLAND V WEST INDIES, WORLD T20 FINAL – KOLKATA, APRIL 2016

West Indies needed 19 off the final over or the trophy was England's. Ben Stokes had the ball in his hand, bowling to big all-rounder Carlos Brathwaite. It was a big ask for a young man to get the chasing team over the line... Six. Six. Six. Six. Job done with two balls to spare. Stokes? He'd be back. But this was a horror show. ∎

Nightmare Seasons

COUNTY CAMPAIGNS THAT STARTED BADLY AND GOT WORSE

10) YORKSHIRE 1984

The centre of the county's universe for the best part of two decades, Geoff Boycott dominated all things Yorkshire cricket across the Seventies and Eighties... good and bad. Most notably under "bad" was the string of events that followed from the General Committee's decision, in October 1983, not to offer Boycott a contract for 1984 despite granting him a testimonial season just three months previously. Unsurprisingly, Boycott was having none of the Committee's attempts to placate him with a series of celebratory "exhibition" matches and, after much wrangling, he duly secured the contract he craved, while the Committee resigned en masse. The fires had been doused, but the months of turmoil had shaken the club and, under the stewardship of David Bairstow, Yorkshire stumbled to a 14th-place finish, winning just five of 24 matches. Perhaps most depressing for the membership, however, was the sheer dreariness of Boycott's batting. Never one to go off like a firecracker, old "Fiery" surpassed himself as a season's average of 62.68 was achieved with a dour scoring rate of 1.32 runs per over. A tally of 1,567 runs in 1,187 overs: that's not entertainment.

9) SURREY 1940 (–1945)

War's not fun for anyone, and whilst Hitler's henchmen were dropping bombs all over London town, cricket also suffered at the hands of the Führer. It was decided that London's two major grounds would be turned into POW camps. While Lord's was eventually spared, allowing MCC to stage many public-school and representative games throughout the war, The Oval was transformed for the purpose, with the pavilion also employed as a furniture store. In the event, the ground – soon a maze of concrete posts and wire – was never used but the outfield had been badly damaged and considerable repair work was necessary in subsequent years.

8) SOMERSET 1986

Having won the NatWest Bank Trophy in 1983, Somerset finished bottom of the Championship in 1985 and next-to-bottom the following year. Two years of underachievement had obviously taken their toll, tensions reaching boiling point when new captain Peter Roebuck advised their West Indian stars, Viv Richards (who would later accuse Roebuck of treachery) and Joel Garner, that they would not be offered contract renewals for the 1987 season. An apoplectic Ian Botham warned Roebuck that he had "better stay away from him", before refusing a new contract and heading off to Worcester.

7) WORCESTERSHIRE 1919

While recent times have seen New Road occasionally resemble a swimming pool, Worcestershire's dampest squib of a season came immediately after the cessation of the Great War. The club's finances were in such a dire way in 1919 that they felt unable to put a side out in the County Championship and they managed just two first-class matches across the season. The culmination of a financial slide that had come to a head in 1913, an investigation of the finances revealed that the club had been operating at a loss every year since gaining first-class status.

6) DERBYSHIRE 1997

In 1996, Derbyshire, led by Victorian Dean Jones, secured their best-ever Championship finish, ending the season as runners-up to Leicestershire with nine victories and just three defeats across the summer. However, despite the unprecedented success, discord was never far from a dressing-room containing former captain Kim Barnett (who would later be a major player in the notorious stand-off between then-captain Dominic Cork and the 14-strong club committee) and Jones (a man known for his abrasive nature and caustic remarks). After a poor start to the '97 season, relations quickly deteriorated with matters coming to a head on 8 June. Led by Barnett, the dressing-room mutinied, Jones resigned and Australian coach, Les Stilman, was relegated to second-team duties before disappearing to Venice. In the wake of this upheaval, the side registered just two wins to finish a miserable 16th. Infighting and Derbyshire were the best of friends for some years hence.

5) ESSEX 2001

Promoted the previous season, in 2001 Essex finished rock bottom of Division One with only two wins to their name. Poor showings in the Sunday League and B&H Cup completed a season of on-field disappointment but it was ructions off the pitch that hit the headlines and threatened to undermine the very fabric of the club. Despite a glittering six seasons with Essex, star batsman Stuart Law left mid-season after a protracted and very public row with his teammates, complaining of a perceived lack of respect from within the dressing-room, and senior players, Mark Illot and Paul Prichard, also voiced their concerns about the direction of the side. That all 23 members of the playing staff were out of contract at the end of the year – and not informed of their fate until mid-September – hardly helped the mood within the camp. Below-par seasons from Ronnie Irani (who had been in sparkling form in 2000) and the promising Stephen Peters (who managed just one half-century in 25 innings) were typical of the team's lacklustre and luckless year. After 20 years of success at Chelmsford, the boom years had finally bust.

4) NOTTINGHAMSHIRE 1881

This is the only instance of county players going on strike. Notts' seven "Test" players demanded benefits written into their contracts and a guaranteed place in what was, at the time, the best county side in the land. Having seen the touring Australians cash in through the staging of some lucrative matches in 1880, the "rebels", led by star bowler Alfred Shaw, quickly fell out with the club (who disapproved of their money-making schemes) and refused to sign contracts tying them in to Notts' official programme of matches for upcoming summer. And while all seven played in the first game of the season, against Sussex at the end of May, the dispute rumbled on until 1882 and Notts spent most of the summer fielding a virtual second XI.

3) DURHAM 2016

As the 2016 season drew to a close, Durham could look back with a degree of contentment, and forward with some hope. While they had lost two of their best batsmen, Mark Stoneman and Scott Borthwick, to Surrey, and suffered defeat in the NatWest T20 Blast final. They could take pride in their unmatched record of never having been relegated from Division One, and had been buoyed by the return to action of Mark Wood, England's fastest bowler, after ankle surgery. Fast-forward a month, and the outlook was considerably less rosy. A devastated Wood discovered he had broken the joint in his ankle and would miss England's winter tours. Meanwhile the club, as punishment for having to accept a bailout from the ECB, were relegated, handed multiple points-deductions and prize-money penalties, and found their future existence thrown into doubt.

2) DERBYSHIRE 1886

So abject were the Peakites in the 1880s that the press effectively ousted them from the County Championship. Although they played first-class matches, the media of the day turned a blind eye, refusing to enter the club's name in the Championship table or to put any of the club's players in the national averages. Two years later, on the back of some disastrous performances, they lost their first-class status, finally regaining admission to the Championship in 1895.

1) NORTHAMPTONSHIRE 1935 (–1939)

From halfway through the 1935 campaign to the mid-point of the 1939 season, Northants failed to win a single game. Bankrolled by Lord Lilford (a veteran of one match for the county and president for 18 years) throughout this dankest of dank spells, what amounted to four whole 30-match seasons passed without victory as the club finished last every year between 1934 and 1938. A win over lowly Leicestershire (by a whopping margin of an innings and 193 runs) finally ended the losing streak, but they weren't to taste victory again that summer and, with war interrupting, it was to be their last win until 1946. ∎

Glenn McGrath
gets his man…
again

Bunnies

SOMETIMES YOU JUST CAN'T EXPLAIN WHY
SOMEONE'S GOT THE WOOD OVER YOU

10) TIM LAMB ON DAVID GOWER

Pure Gower. County cricket was just too dry for a batsman whose juices flowed best with the champers on a blazing Lord's Saturday – of his 53 first-class centuries, 18 of them came in Tests. So it was apt that the man who knocked him over whenever Gower was inconvenienced by the county treadmill was Tim Lamb, a paceless Northants seamer (and future chief executive of the ECB) of mild potency. Lamb's apologetic wobblers dismissed him eight times for fewer than 50, getting him lbw for nought twice in one particular match on the distinctly un-Goweresque stage of Wantage Road, Northampton. See it as a gift from the great man to the little people.

9) HANSIE CRONJE ON SACHIN TENDULKAR

If the cricketing gods had any moral decency, the angel from Mumbai would have cast a silky veil over Cronje's dastardly efforts. But no, instead the South African's medium-wobblers consistently accounted for Sachin throughout his career: "Honestly," Tendulkar explained, "I got out to Hansie more than anyone. He always got me out more than Allan Donald or Shaun Pollock. It wasn't that I couldn't pick him, it's just that the ball seemed to go straight to a fielder." Eight times in all, five in Tests, three times in pyjamas. The divinities, as ever, were in mischievous mood.

8) BHAGWATH CHANDRASEKHAR ON VIV RICHARDS

It's hard to imagine the great man being subdued by anyone, but the twirly, bony mysticism of India's pre-eminent leggie was often too much for Sir Viv. Although Richards fell to Chandrasekhar just four times in Tests, the Indian spinner's variations reduced him to mere competence. Sir Viv later conceded that, after Dennis Lillee, it was Chandrasekhar who gave him the most problems in his Test career.

7) MORNE MORKEL ON ANDREW STRAUSS

Though a brilliant player of pace during his career, Andrew Strauss could never quite escape the clutches of South Africa's wordless Karloffian monster Morne Morkel. Strauss averaged just 21 in Tests when Morkel's rib-bothering angle of attack featured. The quick's amiable viciousness finally did for the English general in the 2012 summer, nailing him on the back leg in the first over of the Test series to set the final ball rolling. That lbw at The Oval was the eighth time Morkel had got him out in Tests. With its echoes of those one-sided youth v age contests from the bad old days (Michael Holding pinning Brian Close; Jeff Thomson bouncing Colin Cowdrey), it confirmed once again – just in case anyone was in any doubt – that sometimes cricket just isn't reasonable.

6) ANDRE NEL ON BRIAN LARA

No single bowler ever dominated Lara. Not Warne nor McGrath, nor Donald, nor Kumble. But Andre Nel's alter ego – an oxygen-starved German with a short fuse who lives in the mountains – got close. "Gunther" ("He takes me over," says Nel) cut Lara down eight times in Tests and on three occasions in ODIs, with the West Indian too freaked out by the bounding vision of a camp, seven-foot wild man to concentrate. You could hardly blame him. It's probably worth pointing out that Lara still averaged over 100 in the matches in which Gunther lurked.

5) ANDREW FLINTOFF ON ADAM GILCHRIST

It was perhaps the single biggest factor in England's 2005 Ashes triumph. Adam Gilchrist had done some terrible things to England in the past. It was assumed he was unstoppable. But that summer he didn't reach 50 in ten innings. This was down primarily to a raging northern fire coming around the wicket, going after the ribs and seeking out the outside edge. Andrew Flintoff got him out four times that series, leaving the great destroyer so shrunken by the "intense and personal" humiliation that it left him questioning his desire and aptitude for the game. He needn't have worried. During the next series that he faced England, he hit a 57-ball hundred at Perth. Turns out he could play after all.

4) YUVRAJ SINGH ON KEVIN PIETERSEN

The "pie-chucker" with his "left-arm filth" has been the butt of a few good-natured barbs from KP in his time, but the banter barely masks Pietersen's troubles against Yuvraj Singh's canny lobs. Four times in ODI cricket KP fell to him, playing inside and out, angled bat and all.

3) TERRY ALDERMAN ON GRAHAM GOOCH

This was an old-world tussle with only one winner. Terry and Graham, Graham and Terry: inseparable through much of the Eighties; more specifically, Terry's in-ducker would rub up intimately against Graham's showy front pad. It began in 1981, when Gooch kept playing round straight deliveries, and the affair was resurrected in '89, when Australia's plan and Gooch's inability to resist it reached almost comic levels. Towards the end of that series England's mustachioed daddy had quietly asked if he could be dropped.

2) GLENN MCGRATH ON MICHAEL ATHERTON

Probably the most famous bunny of them all. It's almost too painful to go over again but no list of bunnies is complete without the tale of Atherton's 19 nervous breakdowns against McGrath. It seemed to crystallise England's inferiority complex during the era: our best boy would walk out, take guard, try and clear his head of the previous day-and-a-half, survey the field, block out Warne's latest wisecrack, take a half-step forward, prod at McGrath's seamer and, feeling the nick, jackrabbit behind to catch the ball sinking miserably into Healy's smug gloves. This was the Nineties.

1) SHANE WARNE ON DARYLL CULLINAN

Warne may have stored up more bunnies than Hugh Hefner, but of all his many victims his most cherished acquisition had to be poor Daryll Cullinan. The South African was one of the most assured technicians of the mid-Nineties, an all-round player with three Test tons on turning Asian pitches, but Warne landed him up in counselling. Cullinan averaged 2.75 in four Tests against Warne's Australia. He may have been clueless against his variations – he would later concede that "quite simply, Warne was too good for me" – but at least he didn't lose the power of speech. When Warne greeted him for the first Test of a series in South Africa with the pleasantry that he'd been "waiting two years for this opportunity to humiliate you in front of your own crowd," Cullinan replied: "Looks like you spent it eating." ∎

The New Bothams

10) DEREK PRINGLE

Test debut: 1982

30 Tests (70 wickets; one fifty), 44 ODIs (44 wickets; 0 fifties)

Broad of beam and the first English Test cricketer to sport an earring, Pringle had the physique and the rebellious streak to fill Botham's shoes, and was duly thrown into an Ashes tour in 1982/83 before he'd sobered up from Cambridge. Indeed, the classical education didn't quite match up with the burly image. He later bowled usefully alongside Botham in the '92 World Cup.

9) PHIL DEFREITAS

Test debut: 1986

44 Tests (140 wickets; four fifties), 103 ODIs (115 wickets; one fifty)

DeFreitas was measured for the crown after the 1986/87 Ashes tour, when pundits figured that if the young pup could survive three months as Botham's room-mate, he was capable of anything. At his best, Daffy's away-swingers evoked the Beefster somewhere near his pomp. One stunning knock at Adelaide in 1994/95 left us wondering what might have been, but though that 95-ball 88 led to a great England victory, the innings remained his highest Test score.

8) DAVID CAPEL

Test debut: 1987

15 Tests (21 wickets; two fifties), 23 ODIs (17 wickets; one fifty)

A plucky fifty against Imran and Wasim on debut promised much, but Capel never quite shook the backhanded "plucky" compliment, and after 15 Tests he was dispensed with. It was harsh treatment of a good cricketer who would go on to take over 500 first-class wickets and make over 12,000 runs. Clean-bowling Viv Richards at Barbados in 1990 hinted at a Botham-esque love of the big moment; being hit out of the park by Gordon Greenidge a week later in Antigua kept the excitement in perspective.

7) CHRIS LEWIS

Test debut: 1990

32 Tests (93 wickets; one hundred, four fifties), 53 ODIs (66 wickets; 0 fifties)

Chris Lewis could have been a contender. On the good days he bowled fast and straight with a beautifully fluid action, fielded like no other English cricketer and struck the ball with freedom and power. But the good days were just too infrequent, and the sweet memories – clean-bowling Sachin at Lord's, smashing a century at Chennai, a key role in the 1992 World Cup – were eventually lost underneath a pile of ill-advised trysts, from nude magazine shoots, to getting sunstroke on England duty, to iffy excuses for being late. That he later found himself in a prison cell in Sutton serving time after a cocaine-trafficking bust makes for a sad footnote.

6) DERMOT REEVE

Test debut: 1993

3 Tests (two wickets; one fifty), 29 ODIs (20 wickets; 0 fifties)

Another member of the 1992 World Cup squad, Dermot Reeve fancied himself as a new Botham. Something rotten. However, a total of 20 wickets and 291 runs from 29 ODIs speaks for itself. But as Warwickshire's club captain in the Nineties, he was something of a phenomenon. Later he moved into a career as a fabulously erratic TV commentator.

5) DARREN GOUGH
Test debut: 1994
58 Tests (229 wickets; two fifties), 159 ODIs (235 wickets; 0 fifties)

For what seemed at least six minutes in 1994, Darren Gough was not merely England's best fast-bowling hope in a generation, he was being proclaimed as Ian Botham reincarnate. This was thanks to a riotous half-century on debut against New Zealand in 1994 and some inspired thwacking at Sydney later that winter. If the Eighties were Botham's, then the Nineties (as much as they belonged to any Englishman) were Dazzler's. But after that knock at Sydney, he never made another fifty in his Test career.

4) CRAIG WHITE
Test debut: 1994
30 Tests (59 wickets; one hundred, five fifties), 51 ODIs (65 wickets; one fifty)

Craig White's career with England can be split into two categories. The "Sleepy" period, 1994–97, as a defensive back-up bowler and chippy No.6. And the "Wheels" era of 2000–02, when he found another gear, sent down some rapid spells (bowling Lara around his legs in 2000), and smacked it about with the bat. His body gave way midway through an Ashes series in Australia, but for two fiery years he had given a damn good impression of a charismatic international all-rounder. Beefy has had worse pretenders.

3) DOMINIC CORK
Test debut: 1995
37 Tests (131 wickets; three fifties), 32 ODIs (41 wickets; 0 fifties)

He certainly had the ego; he may even have had the big-match temperament. Indeed, for a couple of years in the mid-Nineties, around the time that Cork was cutting the West Indians to pieces – something Botham never quite managed – it appeared that England may have finally found their man. But Cork's ebullience couldn't disguise his limitations with the bat at Test level, and with the ball in foreign conditions he couldn't find the late movement that had first got people talking. A good England career that certainly had its moments came to an end in 2002.

2) BEN HOLLIOAKE

Test debut: 1999

Two Tests (four wickets; 0 fifties), 20 ODIs (eight wickets; two fifties)

Ben Hollioake was just 19 when he first strolled out to bat for England. Even then, in 1997, this willowy Anglo-Australian was already a dangerous cricketer, a supremely clean ball-striker and a bowler with a strong, high action whose natural athleticism spoke of great things for the future. And at Lord's that day, against Australia in the final ODI of the pre-Ashes series, the teenager would play one of the great cameo innings in the history of the old ground. His 63 featured a languid six against Warne, some upright drives against McGrath and enough sprinkling of class to leave us intrigued. Two months later he was in the Test team.

But Hollioake would not get to fulfil his promise. On the night of 23 March 2002, in Perth, Western Australia, he lost control of his Porsche as he drove back from a family meal. It span off the road and straight into a wall. He died, aged just 24 years and 132 days. He was the youngest English Test cricketer to die. At his funeral, Alec Stewart described Ben as the most naturally gifted cricketer that he had ever played with.

1) ANDREW FLINTOFF

Test debut: 1998

79 Tests (226 wickets; five hundreds, 26 fifties), 141 ODIs (169 wickets; three hundreds, 18 fifties)

It started meekly with a scratchy 17 and a pair, and finished hobbling on one leg, with just a bullet arm to call upon. But for four years between 2003 and 2006 Flintoff justified his place in England's Test team on batting or bowling alone. In order to end our obsessive quest for the "New Botham", it had fallen on Flintoff to make the game loveable again, and in 2005 Fred did just that. He changed the perception of cricket in England, and took it onto another plane – just as Botham had 24 years before him. ∎

Chris Lewis never made the most of his abundant talent

Ian Botham gets the
silent treatment from
the MCC faithful

Ugly Ducks

INFAMOUS NOUGHTS FROM THE ANNALS

10) IAN BOTHAM

England v Australia, Lord's, 1981

"I'll show you, you bastards." This was Botham's first thought as the then-England captain sloped past the Lord's members having bagged his second duck of the match. Looking for quick runs to set up a declaration, Botham had just been bowled round his legs going for a big sweep, but it was the stony reaction that really got the man riled. Relations between Beef and the blazers would never fully recover as Botham was removed as captain at the end of the match. Still, the next Test was at Headingley. Beefy had a point to prove. It's fair to say he made it.

9) MANINDER SINGH

India v Australia, Madras, 1986

As a man who racked up 11 blobs in 38 Test innings at an average of 3.80, India's guileful twirler was not unaccustomed to batting disappointment, and his woeful willow-wielding took its place in history when for the second time in 1,052 matches a Test finished tied. After Ravi Shastri stole a single to leave the scores level, Maninder had two deliveries from Greg Matthews to negotiate. "I was positive I could get the single and win the match," said Maninder. His optimism was admirable but ultimately unfounded as he was trapped in front to leave the scores all-square.

8) GRAHAM GOOCH
England v Australia, Edgbaston, 1975

In life, "a pair" equals togetherness, companionship, shared experience. From love to trousers, a pair is best. Except in cricket. In cricket a pair means pain, squared. It's the lowest of the low for a batsman. Not only incapable of edging one onto the thigh pad for a filthy scampered single, but incapable twice. Graham Gooch picked up a pair on his Test debut – the second duck a dirty strangle down the leg side – and only played one more match before being cast out for three years. He did okay when he came back, mind...

7) PETER JUDGE
Glamorgan v India, Cardiff Arms Park, 1946

The former RAF pilot and Glamorgan paceman takes his place in this list by virtue of being dismissed for nought twice, by successive deliveries from Indian offie Chandu Sarwate, all inside a minute. After Judge was last man out in Glamorgan's first innings the tourists enforced the follow-on and, with little time left in the day, skipper Johnnie Clay decided to give the home crowd some entertainment, reversing the batting order and waiving the ten-minute interval between innings. Judge stayed where he was, took a fresh guard, and was promptly bowled again.

6) VIRENDER SEHWAG
England v India, Edgbaston, 2011

Having been royally thumped in the first two Tests, India were banking on the return of their most formidable weapon to turn the tables in the battle to be crowned the world's No.1 Test side.

Sehwag was coming in cold after a shoulder injury and looked to be carrying a few extra pounds, but MS Dhoni was backing his heavy artillery to fire. "He just needs to play his natural game," said the Indian captain at the toss. Sehwag took his skipper's advice in the most literal sense. After gloving behind in the first dig, he wafted wildly in the second to become the 13th batsman to register a king pair in Tests.

5) DON BRADMAN
England v Australia, The Oval, 1948

This was the most famous and emotionally overwrought nought of all time, and all the grander for it. Bradman, the machine, was rendered so floppy and tearful by the ovation that greeted his final march to the middle in a Test match that he could barely take guard after all the pats and handshakes. "I don't expect to get a wicket," said John Arlott on commentary, as he settled himself in. Bradman famously needed four for a career average of 100. "Hollies tosses the ball up slowly, and... he's... bowled?" Arlott the great orator was stunned into a 15-second silence, as were the England team. Finally Arlott gathered himself: "Bradman. Bowled. Hollies. Nought. Bowled Hollies. Nought. What can you say?" So much more poetic to retire on 99.94, the moment proved the machine was human after all.

4) JOHN ABRAHAMS
Lancashire v Warwickshire, Lord's, 1984

Man of the Match for captaincy? "For holding his nerve in impossibly tight situations, for making pinpoint calls at just the right time and for waving his arms about convincingly, the award goes to Lancashire's inspirational leader, John Abrahams..." Never mind that he hadn't bowled a ball or managed to score a run, bagging a duck to leave Lancashire tottering on 71 for 4 chasing 139, his stewardship was clearly a triumph of Churchillian magnitude over and above any such vulgar act as someone actually doing something.

3) KEITH MILLER
Essex v Australia, Southend, 1948

Disgusted by his captain's insatiable lust for runs and instinctively on the side of the paying public, the great entertainer Keith Miller walked out against Essex with the scoreboard reading 364 for 2. The crowd was restless, bored and uppity. Bradman had already notched his century, and three others would follow suit in a ridiculous final total of 721 from 129 overs. But in the midst of the slaughter Miller was merciful, shouldering arms to his first delivery from Trevor Bailey and allowing himself to be bowled. Seeing the stumps broken, Miller turned to the Essex wicketkeeper and said, "Thank God that's over."

2) PETER SUCH
England v New Zealand, Old Trafford, 1999

"Screaming" Pete Such may be better known these days as the ECB's head spin-coach, but in his pomp he was a purveyor of beautiful off-breaks and thrillingly inept batsmanship. As the sporadic clown-soldier of Nineties England's lower-order, Such briefly threatened Eddie the Eagle's position as England's favourite sporting have-a-go hero, with an irresistible concoction of cluelessness and courage. The Old Trafford crowd watched him block, grope at, wear and swallow 51 balls for no return against New Zealand in what ended up as his last Test match, before he waddled off to a raucous standing ovation from the Manchester faithful.

1) VIV RICHARDS
Antigua v St Kitts, St John's Recreation Ground, 1969

The boy-genius was already the angel of Antigua. Selected for the national side as a 17-year-old, 6,000 locals came out in force. Viv went in No.3, "verbally assaulting" – his words – the opposition as he walked out. So cocky was Viv that when his first delivery popped up to short-leg and the umpire raised the finger, the boy refused to shift. Only after a few moments did he start to drag himself off, by which time the crowd had turned restive. The authorities panicked. In an extraordinary move, they reinstated him – but the boy, spangled by this point, was duly stumped first ball. In the second innings he bagged another nought – his third of the match. Finally, the authorities who had earlier insisted he return to the field to bat again, slapped him with a two-year ban for dissent. Richards served his time, learnt how to box, and returned with a ton for Antigua in his comeback match. ∎

Michael Atherton
was cruelly denied
a century at Lord's

Run Out Ninety-Nines

IF GETTING RUN OUT IS THE WORST FEELING IN CRICKET, THEN IMAGINE THE AGONY OF GETTING CAUGHT SHORT ON 99

10) JASON GALLIAN 199
(Twice!) 2005 county season

Oscar Wilde once quipped: "To lose one parent may be regarded as a misfortune; to lose both looks like carelessness." It's the kind of gallows humour that may have helped Nottinghamshire's Jason Gallian reconcile the calamity of being run out – incredibly – for 199 not once but twice in the same county season. A phlegmatic Gallian reflected: "I couldn't believe it had happened again... I was laughing. It was just one of those situations, going for some quick runs to try to make the most of our total and win the game."

9) GRAHAM GOOCH 99
Australia v England, 3rd Test, MCG, 1980

England's former batting coach Graham Gooch is well known for his insistence that "daddy hundreds" are what players should strive for – in fact Alastair Cook once remarked: "He doesn't count it if it's under 150." But Goochie didn't always adhere to that philosophy during his own playing career. Such was his eagerness to reach his maiden Test century, a full five years after his debut, Gooch absurdly ran himself out for 99 in the final over before tea.

8) YOUNUS KHAN 199
Pakistan v India, 1st Test, Lahore, 2006

The first Test between Pakistan (679 for 7) and India (410 for 1) at Lahore in 2006 could lay claim to being the dullest Test match of all time. Of the 12 batsmen who had a knock in the match, half made centuries. The monotony, however, was briefly broken on day two when Younus Khan became the first batsman in Test history to be run out for 199. Driving to mid-on, the unfortunate Younus found his partner, a slumberous Shahid Afridi, with his back turned on the action and was undone by a direct hit as he tried to scamper back. In the context of the match, you can't really blame Afridi for snoozing.

7) DON BRADMAN 299*
Australia v South Africa, 4th Test, Adelaide, 1932

As The Don approached his second Test triple-century he found himself with only debutant No.11 Hugh "Pud" Thurlow for company. With Bradman desperate to retain the strike, Thurlow was run out for a duck, leaving Bradman stranded on 299. While the senior man graciously accepted responsibility at the time (the not-out helped him average 201.50 in the series), conspiracy theorists may note that Thurlow never played another Test match.

6) MS DHONI 99
India v England, 4th Test, Nagpur, 2012

Runs are something we've come to expect from Alastair Cook; one-handed swooping pick-ups and direct hits are not. But that was exactly how the England skipper dismissed his opposite number during the 2012 Nagpur Test. It was a pivotal moment, stopping India in their tracks, and helped England secure an unlikely first-innings lead and ultimately secure the series as Dhoni became the first Test captain ever to be run out for 99.

5) VIRAT KOHLI 99
Delhi Daredevils v Royal Challengers Bangalore, IPL match, Delhi, 2013

Virat Kohli agonisingly missed out on a first T20 century by a single run during the 2013 IPL. Having bludgeoned 22 runs from the first five balls of the final over, Kohli required two runs from the last ball of the innings to bring up three figures. He smashed the ball out to deep-point to give himself every chance, but a fine pick-up and throw from Ben Rohrer saw him well short of his ground, thus becoming the first player in IPL history to be run out for 99.

4) SANATH JAYASURIYA 99
Sri Lanka v England, VB Series ODI, Adelaide, 2003

Nasser Hussain was involved in a few farcical run-outs during his career but surely none were as comical as that of Sanath Jayasuriya at Adelaide in 2003. Chasing England's 279 for 6, the Sri Lankan left-hander had advanced to 99 in just the 28th over when disaster struck. Having driven to Hussain at mid-off for a comfortable single, Jayasuriya and partner Kumar Sangakkara gravely took the same route down the pitch, running wider and wider and wider still, magnetically pulled into a collision at short mid-wicket. Despite completing about 24 yards with the angle, the opener was still three yards short when Nasser's throw hit the stumps.

3) HANIF MOHAMMAD 499
Karachi v Bahawalpur, Quaid-e-Azam Trophy semi-final, Karachi, 1959

On 11 January 1959 the original "Little Master", Hanif Mohammad, was run out just one shy of 500. Wanting to give his captain the option of declaring overnight, Mohammad fatally ran on a misfield from the penultimate ball of the day and missed out on the chance of becoming the first man to rack up a quintuple century. "I thought I was gone for 497, but as I walked back the scoreboard showed 499! I would never have pushed so hard if I knew I was on 498 and not 496." He quickly got over it, though. "499 is better than most scores," he said.

2) STEVE WAUGH 99*
Australia v England, 5th Test, Perth, 1995

It's said batsmen who spend long periods together can develop a telepathic understanding. Add into the mix the supposed extrasensory abilities of twins, and surely the Waugh brothers would be the perfect partners when it came to judging a quick single, right? Wrong. At Perth in 1995, Steve Waugh was left stranded on 99 not out when brother Mark (acting as a runner for last man Craig McDermott) inexplicably charged down the wicket despite Steve hitting the ball straight back to the bowler, and was run out at the non-striker's end.

1) MICHAEL ATHERTON 99
England v Australia, 2nd Test, Lord's, 1993

"Oh tragedy, tragedy!" Not the words of Barry Gibb or "H" from Steps, but those of the Beeb's Tony Lewis as Michael Atherton desperately crawled along the turf four yards short of his ground. While the famous slope has undone many a batsman over the years, the imaginary banana skin has claimed significantly fewer victims. But here, as Merv Hughes' throw arrived from deep mid-wicket, young Athers, having been sent back by Mike Gatting, went sprawling. He missed out on a place on the honours board by a single run and – unlike Jacob Oram, Tamim Iqbal and Matt Horne – never made a Test hundred at Lord's. ■

The Ugly

Cricket, like most drama queens, is obsessed with food, bodies and hair. Look around you. Are there any professional cricketers left who haven't undergone a little sponsored barnet-replenishment? Will Mike Gatting's immortal cheese roll ever get tired? Or will he, it, and the notion of "a little extra timber" continue to bedazzle us all for centuries to come? Will we ever fail to be amazed by cricketers who are quite tall or quite fat or quite small? And the big one: can we ever rest until Derek Pringle's in a toboggan on primetime Channel 5? These are the questions of our times. In this section you will find all the star-spangled absurdities and excessive vanities of our beloved heroes. Forget what happens on the pitch, with all those runs and wickets and so on. Wait until you get them peering out of a tiny newspaper advert looking sad and bald one minute, raffishly hirsute the next. Then, and only then, can a man truly reveal himself.

Infamous Interviews

AWKWARD INTERVIEWS THAT WON'T
EASILY BE FORGOTTEN

10) WARNER STINKS OUT THE GABBATOIR

Jonathan Trott was not in a good place at Brisbane in November 2013, England were taking the first step towards a humiliating whitewash, and David Warner was keen to remind them of this. "It does look like they have got scared eyes at the moment." Alright, mate. "The way Trotty got out today was pretty poor and weak." Enough now, you've made a ton and you're going to win the Test, but steady on. Warner was left red-faced when a couple of days later Trott checked in at Brisbane International.

9) MOORES THE PITY

A World Cup campaign over in 28 days and a reputation for data-driven cricket entrenched. Speaking to the BBC after the defeat to Bangladesh, England's coach Peter Moores appeared to say: "We'll have to look at the data." The internet rose up in fury, but it never happened. Moores had said "later" rather than "data" and, although he did mention data in an interview with Sky, the context was totally different. However, when Moores was sacked six weeks later, this was to be his legacy.

8) GAYLE'S BLOW OUT

On 4 January 2016 Chris Gayle told Aussie reporter Mel McLaughlin not to "blush" during a pitch-side interview. When Cricket Australia took exception to his comments, he dismissed journalists' questions by saying it was all a joke. Fast-forward to May, and Gayle was being interviewed by Charlotte Edwardes of *The Times* when he claimed to have "a very, very big bat, the biggest in the wooooorld," before asking: "You think you could lift it? You'd need two hands." Charm offensive complete.

7) BIG WILLEY STYLE

Jade Dernbach and David Willey may not care to admit it, but they are actually pretty similar characters: fiery, heart-on-sleeve sorts who say it as they see it. We knew Dernbach well by 2013, but Willey was not so familiar. He made a name for himself at T20 Finals day, though: first through his brilliant showing on the pitch, and then by telling the media what he thought of the Surrey paceman. "I don't really like the bloke, to be honest," said Willey. Say what you really think, Dave.

6) BIT OF BEEF

These were the days when men were men, and they said what the hell they thought. These were also the days when Ian Botham was managed by the DJ Tim Hudson, who described the all-rounder as "the greatest British hero since Wellington or Nelson". Somehow – who knows how – Beefy ended up on BBC Scotland in 1986 faced with a panel of exceptionally well-educated teens, and said his piece on a variety of issues. This included fox-hunting ("There are more deer in this country than in the days of King Henry VIII. Fact"), parenting ("If you want to change nappies, change nappies. It's a free world. That's why my father fought in the Second World War") and drugs ("The next thing you know you've got some kid chasing the dragon at the age of 14").

5) BOXING DAY KO

It was the 2013/14 Ashes, Boxing Day, and the series was to all intents and purposes done. Channel 9 decided to give the women's game a five-minute slot in its coverage, as Meg Lanning and Ellyse Perry joined Michaels Slater and Vaughan for a toe-curling chat. Slater middled his opening line – "Hello ladies, you're looking fantastic as always" – before moving on to some patronising patter about the improving skills in the women's game and launching a segue into some pictures of Lanning and Perry modelling swimwear. "Don't be embarrassed," says Slater. Cringe.

4) MARLON'S BAD MANNERS

If there was something noble about Darren Sammy sticking up for his much-maligned team after their World T20 win over England, then Marlon Samuels' feet-on-the-table moment in the post-match presser, funny though it may have been, rather spoiled it. Samuels took aim at his many detractors, opening up with Ben Stokes – "He just doesn't learn" – before tucking into his arch-nemesis Shane Warne. "I don't know [why he doesn't like me], maybe it is because my face is real and his face is not."

3) BIG BOB STICKS THE BOOT IN

"The standard of journalism in this country," Bob Willis (son of a journalist from this country) said to journalists from this country, "has gone down the nick completely." The scene was Headingley '81, and the context meant that Willis could say, well, anything he liked. "People have to rely on small-minded quotes from players under pressure for their stories," he continued. "Where they used to write about cricket, they don't seem to be able to do that any more." That's them told, then.

2) IT'S NOT EASY BEING KP

Headingley again, and another sensational performance, both on and off the field. When Kevin Pietersen proclaimed – after hitting a superb century against South Africa in 2012 – that it "is not easy being me", he was not mouthing off about the media, but his own teammates. In fact, this period of Pietersen's tumultuous career was a triumph of modern media: there were those misguided BBM messages, the infamous parody Twitter account and, of course, that YouTube apology. What a time to be alive.

1) RAGEFUL RAVI

Ravi Shastri had been India's team director between 2014 and 2016 and was very keen on the national coaching role when Duncan Fletcher stepped aside. He gave a video interview to the selection panel, who eventually picked Anil Kumble instead. Shastri didn't take the decision well, directing his anger at Sourav Ganguly who was on the panel but chose not to sit in on his interview. "Nothing surprises me in Indian cricket anymore," he raged. "A member of the committee [Ganguly] wasn't present and that was disrespectful to the selection process. He was disrespectful to the job he was entrusted with." ∎

Fred Trueman's show *The Indoor League* was a big hit in the 70s

TV Vehicles

WHITES, CAMERA, ACTION!

10) DOWN UNDER AND OUT
Warnie

Australian TV network Channel 9 made an attempt to capitalise on Ashes mania by launching Shane Warne's cloying chat show in 2010. The probing questions the legendary leg-spinner asked of batsmen were glaringly absent in his interview technique ("So Danni [Minogue], do you like being a mum?") as Warne repeatedly resisted the urge to throw in a wrong 'un and instead massaged the egos of the rich and famous. Ratings plummeted after a fanfare launch and, by the time Andrew Strauss lifted the urn after the fourth Test, the series had been canned. "I think people were pretty impressed by Shane," said a Channel 9 spokeswoman, "but the reality is that the Ashes was wrapped up after the Melbourne Test so there was no need for the show." Nice swerve.

9) COLD AS ICE
Dancing On Ice

Never one to shirk a challenge, Dominic Cork gallantly took to the ice for the sixth series of ITV's answer to *Strictly* and approached it with typical gusto, despite minimal skating experience. "I love the sequins, the music, the costumes, the lot!" said the former

Derbyshire, Lancashire and Hampshire man. But Corky got a frosty reception from the judging panel. "The thing I like about your performance is when it's over," judge Jason Gardiner told a peeved Cork, who later admitted he wanted to take the Aussie choreographer out back and "give him a smack". Already on thin ice, the former England all-rounder, daubed in a Union Jack waistcoat, delivered a shaky routine to The Who's "I Can See For Miles" and became the sixth contestant to be booted out after falling victim to the dreaded ice pick.

8) LIKE A HOLE IN THE HEAD
Hole In The Wall

After he was crowned champion of *Strictly* in 2005, Darren Gough was briefly hot stuff in the world of Saturday-night TV, and the BBC soon snapped him up as team captain for this ludicrous family gameshow hosted by Dale Winton. In a nutshell, the show saw celebrities attempt to contort themselves to fit through large polystyrene walls that moved towards them. It was magnificently, compellingly awful stuff as Gough desperately writhed on the floor in an unsuccessful attempt to burst balloons attached to his person so he could fit through a matchstick-thin hole before being sent flying into a swimming pool.

7) GONE FISHIN'
Botham On The Fly

Having appeared as a contentedly mulleted team captain for several years on *A Question of Sport*, Ian Botham branched out to present his own programme about his passion for fly-fishing in 2005. He was joined by celebrity guests including such luminaries as Chris Tarrant but – despite the show's grave promise to "not only capture the relationship between Ian and his guest but also provide factual and anecdotal information about each river and its fly-fishing history" – the public never really took the bait.

6) SOUL MAN
Just The Two Of Us

A recording artist in his own right, Mark Butcher duetted with wailing *Phantom of the Opera* songstress Sarah Brightman in 2007 for the second series of this BBC show, which saw celebrities paired with professional singers and judged by a panel of experts. Butch made it through to the final after impressing with his rendition of "Ain't No Sunshine" (described by none other than Tito Jackson as on a par with the Jackson 5's version – bit harsh) but the former England and Surrey batsman was pipped at the last by *EastEnders* actress Hannah Waterman and wet Wet Wet Wet frontman Marti Pellow. No justice.

5) CAPTAIN PLANET
Freddie Flintoff Versus The World

Rather than kicking his heels after his untimely retirement, Fred decided he fancied a challenge. Never a man to do things by halves, he heaved his creaking bones across the globe to take part in a series of daredevil challenges for this thrill-seeking ITV4 show, including white-water rafting down a waterfall, walking on the wing of an aeroplane during flight, riding a raging bull and cliff-jumping in Acapulco. Not content with taking on the world, he invited a few mates along for the ride and competed against guest stars including former England footballer Dennis Wise and NBA ace Dennis Rodman. Having taken on some of the world's more scary challenges, the idea of then becoming a regular on Sky's comedy panel show *A League of Their Own* – alongside Jack Whitehall, James Corden and Jamie Redknapp – was a doddle.

4) CRACKERJACK CUISINE
Britain's Best Dish

After a short stint as host of flop reality show *Survivor*, silver-tongued talksmith Mark Nicholas swapped the Bocas del Toro archipelago of Panama for the kitchen, finding a comfy home as host of ITV's daytime cookery offering. Dutifully ignoring a tedious format that saw contestants return to cook the same dish every week, the housewives' favourite managed to conjure up the same unbound enthusiasm for steak and kidney pudding as a "crackerjack" cover-drive, and hosted the show for four series before stepping aside.

3) FROM TUFFERS TO TARZAN
I'm A Celebrity… Get Me Out Of Here!

Phil Tufnell was the shock winner of the second series of the ITV reality show in 2003, but those who knew him well weren't at all surprised to see the former England spinner crowned King of the media-manufactured Jungle. "Two weeks of sleeping under cover with a qualified chef catering for your needs and having a regular supply of booze and fags dropped in was luxury for Tuffers, even if he had to do the odd Bush Tucker Trial," said his former England and Middlesex teammate Angus Fraser. It was just the beginning of Tuffers' media career and he has since become a chirpy team captain on *A Question of Sport* and a regular fixture on *Test Match Special*.

2) I'LL SEE THEE
Indoor League

They don't make them like this anymore. Presented by Fred Trueman and produced by Mr Darts himself, Sid Waddell, the legendary England fast bowler would typically open the show with a pint of bitter in one hand and a pipe in the other before contestants took each other on at a variety of pub games, including shove ha'penny, bar billiards and arm-wrestling. Originally aired on regional Yorkshire TV in 1972, it went national the following year and Trueman – whose immortal sign-off, "I'll see thee", became something of a catchphrase – presented the show until this gem was laid to rest in 1977.

1) FANCY FOOTWORK
Strictly Come Dancing

Not so very long ago the thought of a professional cricketer appearing on TV in a frilly, sequinned outfit and baring his chest and soul while performing the paso doble would have caused something of a stir, but no more. Darren Gough was the first to break the mould, displaying unexpected panache to hot-step his way to the series three title. Mark Ramprakash followed in Dazzler's immaculate footsteps to leave grown women swooning and made it back-to-back wins for the cricketing fraternity. Never one to miss a media opportunity, the ubiquitous Tuffers jumped aboard the bandwagon but unfortunately didn't show the same flair for the rumba as he did for masticating on maggots and was given his marching orders in week nine. When Michael Vaughan followed Tuffers' lead in 2012, and left at the halfway stage of the show (despite a high-scoring American Smooth), cricket's *Strictly* stranglehold was finally loosened. ∎

CRICKET AU

John Buchanan: the
wacky professor

Crickileaks

SOMETIMES, INFORMATION JUST GETS OUT...

10) LANGER DROPS A CLANGER

Justin Langer – once described by Matthew Hoggard as a "brown-nosed gnome" – has always been adept at Pom-baiting, but he unintentionally took it up a notch in the lead-up to the 2013 Ashes when a private email to Aussie coach Tim Nielsen found its way to the *Daily Telegraph*. The dossier critiquing England's squad described Anderson as a "bit of a pussy", Strauss as a "conservative" captain and, most insulting of all, Swann as "on a par with Nathan Hauritz". Langer said he was "shattered" by the leak, while England – no doubt with the dossier pinned to the changing-room wall – won their third Ashes series on the bounce. Not too shabby for a team that, according to Langer, "rarely believe in themselves".

9) NO FAN OF IRFAN

MS Dhoni had enjoyed the smoothest of starts to international captaincy until details of a selection meeting were leaked to the Indian press during England's 2008 tour. The leak was particularly damaging as it alleged Dhoni had offered to step down as captain when the selectors insisted Irfan Pathan be selected ahead of RP Singh, one of Dhoni's closest friends, in the next ODI at Bangalore. "It is disgusting and disrespectful," said the Indian skipper. "You don't want RP to feel that I will go out of the way and stand and defend him, and Irfan should not feel I don't want him in the team." Irfan played the final match of the series – returning figures of 0 for 57 – and was dropped from the side soon after.

8) SKYPEY HAPPY PEOPLE

Before the technological age it was much easier to keep a private conversation private. This meant that if you wanted to blackmail your former lover, you might just have been able to get away with it. How Bangladeshi seamer Rubel Hossain must have wished he lived in a simpler time. After a fall-out with ex-girlfriend Naznin Akter Happy, Rubel took to Skype to tell her that private photographs of her would find their way into the public sphere if she wasn't careful. Happy, happily enough, recorded it all and Rubel's skulduggery was brought to light. Bad man.

7) WARLORDS! WHAT ARE THEY GOOD FOR?

During the 2001 Ashes a team-briefing document was leaked in which Australia's kooky former coach John Buchanan adapted the teachings of fifth-century Chinese military leader Sun Tzu to inspire his troops ahead of combat. Handwritten on two A4 pages, Buchanan noted that Sun Tzu's principles "hold true for most 'battles'" before giving a cricket-specific take on "The Nine Situations" from *The Art of War*. The English press couldn't contain their mirth, but Buchanan had the last laugh as Australia dismantled Nasser Hussain's side with military precision.

6) BENAUD SPILLS THE BEANS

A rain-sodden tour match at Hove during the '77 Ashes gave Ian Wooldridge of the *Daily Mail* a chance to investigate rumours that had been percolating of a rebel league. On a whim, he got on the blower to his old pal Richie Benaud to find out the lie of the land, only to have his questions flat-batted. Two hours later, Richie called back and gave Wooldridge an almighty scoop. World Series Cricket, a cash-rich competition offering players substantially higher salaries, would start that winter. Fifteen players – England captain Tony Greig among them – had already signed up and Benaud was a key adviser to Kerry Packer, the Aussie media magnate who founded the competition. "World's top cricketers turn pirate" blared the front page of the *Daily Mail* the following day. Greig, who had helped Packer recruit players, was accused of treachery and sacked by England four days later.

5) SELECTION SUSPICION

Exactly what happened here is unclear, but that's the point. This is the anti-leak. Those in charge were remarkably watertight, almost as if they had reason to avoid transparency. Basil D'Oliveira, as everyone knows, had just kicked the hornet's nest with a brilliant 158 in the final Test of the '68 Ashes and yet, after a six-hour selection meeting at Lord's, the Cape-Coloured all-rounder wasn't in the original party to tour apartheid South Africa, the land of his birth. The decision was reportedly supported by four of the five selectors, but we cannot be sure, because there's no official record. Were minutes ever taken? Did they go missing? They've certainly never materialised. And how convenient that they haven't.

4) THE BEST-LAID PLANS...

Question: what don't you want as the opposition are in the middle of compiling a 279-run stand? Answer: your "plans" to dismiss them being read out live on air. England's forgettable 2006/07 drubbing came with a side-serving of humiliation as the kind gents at ABC read out their bowling plans for Australia, specifically for Matthew Hayden and Andrew Symonds. Previously pinned up on a notice board in the England dressing-room, the plans – which included working on Hayden's "ego" and deemed bouncers to be "essential" against Symonds – evidently didn't work.

3) SHEPHERDING THE KALE

In hindsight, England's hammering in Oz back in 2013/14 was never going to go well. One of the first clues was the infamous leaking of the side's ultra-specific dietary requirements. Sent out to every host venue, the 84-page document, written by ECB's performance nutritionist Chris Rosimus, had some absolute belters in it for those looking to knock England off their mung-bean perch. Screw the narrative, though, the food sounded delicious. No wonder they let Mitch Johnson roll them over – they had lamb and pea kofta kebabs with mint yoghurt waiting for them in the hutch.

2) YOU BRING THE BODY BUT YOU LOSE ESTEEM

A "broken f***en arm"? Give over. How about a Larwood bouncer to the heart? That was the injury that befell Australia captain Bill Woodfull during the Adelaide Test of the 1932/33 Bodyline series. Visibly shaken and dismissed soon after, Woodfull was visited in the changing-room by England team manager Pelham Warner to enquire after his health. The Aussie wasn't in the mood for chitchat. "I do not want to see you, Mr Warner," said Woodfull. "There are two teams out there. One is playing cricket and the other is not." This exchange was leaked to the press – something virtually unheard of at the time – and widely reported the following day. Australia's Jack Fingleton, a part-time journalist, was assumed by many to be the source of the leak, although he later pointed the finger at Don Bradman, who in turn denied it.

1) WHATSAPP, DOOS

When your defence is reduced to arguing that what you said was just "banter", you're already on pretty shaky, Richard Keys-ian ground. For such a meaningless word, it's very often employed to dismiss accusations of having caused offence. For most people in everyday life, there's no evidence. When your "banter" is on BlackBerry Messenger, and it's with your opposition, and it pertains to your teammates, and it's not always complimentary... you're struggling. Back in 2012, Kevin Pietersen messaged South African players including Steyn and Morkel. While the actual content of those messages is still debated, news that he'd done it certainly leaked out – and with it, the golden era was on its last legs. ■

Greg Chappell took matters into his own hands when an invader interrupted play at Eden Park

Indecent Exposures

CRICKET IN THE RAW

10) BODY PAINT

Blighted by injury, Australian cricketer Lee Carseldine decided to retire from first-class cricket in 2011 and concentrate on being a T20 specialist. He then celebrated his subsequent move to Brisbane Heat in the unashamedly in-your-face style that only a T20 specialist can pull off: by dousing himself in body paint – teal to match his side's kit – popping on just a pair of Speedos, walking around Brisbane's Mount Coot-tha lookout and greeting holidaymakers. Why ever not?

9) BALANCED OUT

After the final day of England's drawn Test against India at Trent Bridge in 2014, Gary Ballance chose to enjoy a little bit of what Nottingham's nightlife had to offer. One or two sherbets later and Ballance could be found dancing topless, swirling his shirt above his head, screaming, "I'm not a cricketer tonight. I'm just a drunken bastard."

8) SUPERMARKET SWEEP

Hands up who hasn't got naked, run into a supermarket in Ashford and tried to buy a bottle of vodka? It's become part of our culture, a rite of passage. During Hampshire second XI's match versus Kent second XI in 2013, somebody – and we're naming no names, predominantly because we don't know who it was – did just that. The person in question was believed to be a Hampshire player but the story is slightly ruined by the internal investigation which followed that concluded no player from the club was involved in the prank... but let's not let the facts get in the way of a good story.

7) PRATTING ABOUT

After some less than superb Ashes performances and some iffy semi-naked modelling shots, England all-rounder Chris Lewis wasn't exactly the darling of the media. On the 1993/94 tour of the West Indies things got worse. Arriving in Antigua, Lewis asked teammate Devon Malcolm to shave off all his hair because of the searing heat. But with the Caribbean sun beating down, Lewis suffered severe sunstroke. With no protection on his bonce throughout the week's training, he had to withdraw ahead of the first warm-up match and was famously dubbed the "prat without a hat" by *The Sun*.

6) BARE CHEEK

Not normally one to lose his cool, Greg Chappell mislaid it in a big way when the third streaker of the day interrupted play at Auckland in 1977. Tasked with steering his side to safety having lost both openers cheaply, Chappell was edgily nudging Australia away from danger when the intruder ran past. Chappell grabbed his arm and spanked the man with his Gray-Nicolls bat. The police escorted the streaker away and normality was restored. Chappell's concentration was broken, though, and he misheard Rick McCosker's call for a single soon after the restart and was run out.

5) WHAT A SHARMA

Fans like to come up with unique ways to celebrate their heroes' achievements and in the age of the internet and social media these gifts can be seen around the world in seconds. So when Rohit Sharma scored a world-record 264 in an ODI against Sri Lanka in 2014, tributes from fanatical followers unsurprisingly poured in. However, model Sofia Hayat caused quite the stir when she posted a nude picture of herself on Twitter in honour of his mammoth hitting, captioning the tweet: "Dedicating my nude shoot to Rohit Sharma for his historic score! Well done! This one is for you! Proud day for India!"

4) BRIMSON THE FLASHER

Squad photos. Dull, right? Not if you're Matthew Brimson. The former Leicestershire spinner jazzed up his county's pre-season snap ahead of the 2000 campaign by exposing his phallus. What a pranker! Unfortunately for Brimson nobody saw the offending organ until it was too late so the Leicestershire pages of that year's *Almanack* were infused with a novel penisy charm. Cue red faces all round and an angry *Wisden* editor in the shape of Matthew Engel. "I think if you're going to pull this kind of stunt, you need to be a more competent sportsman than Matthew Brimson – and, frankly, more impressively arrayed," said Engel.

3) BARING IT ALL

Cricketers aren't used to being photographed in only their birthday suits, so Alastair Cook, Stuart Broad and James Anderson posing naked for *Cosmopolitan* magazine's May 2008 issue came as quite a surprise. With merely a cricket bat to protect their modesty, the trio featured in the mag's centre-page spread raising awareness for male cancer. It wasn't actually a nudity debut for future England skipper Cook; he featured in a photoshoot with Emma Sayle and Natalie Sisson – both in just their underwear and body paint – for "The Art of Sport", a calendar by The Sisterhood looking to raise money for charity.

2) THE HACKER'S MIDDLE STUMP

Ian Botham has never been known to shy away from the limelight, but a little bit too much was on show in the summer of 2014 when a tweet from his Twitter account displayed a photo of a penis with an accompanying message asking recipients to tell him what they were thinking. Botham had precedent for showing off his "old man", writing in his autobiography how he unzipped his trousers when bowling to David Boon to try and put him off. Like his playing days, Botham went on the offensive after this snap, disputing the assertion that he posted the image, and putting it down to his account having been hacked.

1) "A FREAKER!"

Back in 1975, having been fired up by several pints of the Tavern's best, oil-tanker chef Michael Angelow stripped off and daringly dashed across the Lord's outfield. Egged on by a bunch of Australians he had recently befriended, and the promise of £20 for his antics, Angelow hopped over the hoardings and past the statuesque security guards. Hurtling towards the Nursery End, Angelow hurdled both sets of stumps to the amusement of the players and umpires before being escorted off at the Mound Stand. Immortalised by *Test Match Special*'s John Arlott as "a freaker" during commentary, Angelow never did get to keep the £20 as a magistrate's court fined him the same amount for his nude display. ∎

Hysterical Overreactions

WHEN PERSPECTIVE GETS FLOGGED
OVER COW CORNER

10) THE TIGER MOTH MOMENT

All hell broke loose during the 1990/91 Ashes when David Gower and John Morris jumped aboard a Tiger Moth biplane during a tour match against Queensland. England had endured a wretched series and morale was non-existent, so after watching the aircraft passing over the ground for the past three days Gower and Morris hatched a plan to bring some much-needed levity to proceedings. Just as Robin Smith reached his century, Gower and his accomplice Morris buzzed over the Carrara ground at a little over 200 feet to celebrate their teammate's return to form. Smith and Allan Lamb happily acknowledged the moment. The England management failed to see the funny side and fined each player the maximum permitted £1,000. Relations between Gower and captain Graham Gooch – never good at the best of times – reached an all-time low. Gower, who had been in sublime form prior to the incident, barely got a run for the rest of the tour, admitting in his autobiography that, "it did not have an uplifting effect on my spirits". He was discarded after just five more Test matches and Morris's brief Test career was over.

9) DIRTY ATHERS

The dirt-in-pocket affair during the 1994 South Africa series provoked outrage in the English press. But the incident appeared to be smoothed over after the TCCB (the forerunner to the ECB) fined Michael Atherton £2,000 for his offence – half for imparting dirt on the ball, and half for lying to the match referee Peter Burge. The ref was still livid with the England skipper's deception though, and later said he would have suspended Atherton for two matches. In the final Test of the summer at The Oval, Burge exacted his revenge. Atherton was struck on the pads first ball of the innings by South African seamer Fanie de Villiers and given out despite a clear inside-edge. Atherton expressed his disappointment with a barely discernable shake of his head as he trudged back to the pavilion and Burge had the ammunition he needed. He fined the England skipper 50 per cent of his match fee for his "dissent".

8) I DON'T THINK YOU'RE READY FOR THIS JELLY

The media reacting hysterically to an England defeat is nothing new, but the brouhaha following the defeat to India at Trent Bridge in 2007 was novel for its subject matter. It wasn't England's batting, bowling or fielding that caused consternation, but rather their unsporting use of confectionary scattered around the crease when India batted. The debate raged so fiercely that Michael Vaughan had to set matters straight. "We did not lose the game because of jellybeans," said the England skipper. But the victim of the "assault", Zaheer Khan, did look full of beans as he ripped through England's batting line-up. Paul Collingwood appeared to be the only one who appreciated the absurdity of it all: "Zaheer wasn't too pleased. I think he prefers the blue ones to the pink ones."

7) BUCKNOR SACKED

The ICC's code of conduct states that to show dissent at an umpire's decision is strictly prohibited. Unless, it seems, you show enough dissent to get him sacked. India's tour of Australia in 2008 was on the verge of implosion, with the visitors threatening to pack their bags after a series of bitter rows. The volatile atmosphere was further intensified by the Indian authorities' fury at umpire Steve Bucknor, who had made several errors in their second Test defeat at the SCG. Something had to break. It was to be the ICC's resolve to follow their own code of conduct. A veteran of over 120 Test matches, Bucknor was the easiest scapegoat and was axed for the third Test as the ICC attempted to defuse the situation. The then-ICC chief executive Malcolm Speed said: "We could have taken a heavy-handed approach, a letter of the law approach. What we need to do is alleviate some of the tension that is focused on this match. I think this gives us an opportunity to move on." Never mind the reputation of one of the most respected figures in the game then.

6) COLLY'S WOBBLE

Paul Collingwood's decision to uphold the appeal that saw New Zealand's Grant Elliot controversially run out in the ODI at The Oval in 2008 after a collision with Ryan Sidebottom was met with righteous indignation by the Kiwis. And understandably so. No laws had been broken but the spirit of the game had been stretched to the limit. But after the England skipper admitted his error – a split-second decision made in a tense finale – and Vettori accepted his apology, the issue should have been done with. Not in UK tabloid world. Collingwood was hit hard, receiving criticism from fellow professionals and little or no support from upstairs. Within six weeks he'd resigned his post as ODI skipper.

5) GATTING'S A GONER

Mike Gatting had few friends at the TCCB following his infamous slanging match with umpire Shakoor Rana during England's 1987 tour of Pakistan. The episode proved a huge embarrassment as relations between England and Pakistan soured and the Foreign Office became involved. Gatting kept the captaincy, but his job was hanging by a thread, and that thread snapped as the press went big on a story that Gatting had invited a barmaid to his hotel room during a Test match versus West Indies. Trial by tabloid was good enough for the TCCB, who now had the excuse they wanted to remove their controversial skipper. "We don't think he made love to the barmaid, but he shouldn't have invited her to his room," said the TCCB, in a classic line straight out of a PR textbook. Made love!

4) THE VERMEULEN TIME BOMB

The former Zimbabwe batsman has always been somewhat erratic. Back in 1996 he was banned from representing his Harare school for walking off with the stumps and locking himself in the changing-room after disagreeing with an umpire's decision. But after he was struck on the head by a bouncer in 2004, Vermeulen's strange behaviour took a turn for the worse. First he saw red in a Lancashire League match in 2006 – hurling a cricket ball into the crowd, brandishing a boundary marker as a weapon, and tearing down an advertising boarding. He was also twice seen banging on the gates of the presidential palace in Harare, demanding to speak to Robert Mugabe. Vermeulen's increasingly bizarre behaviour culminated in his arrest in 2007 for setting fire to the offices of the Harare Sports Club and the National Academy. He pleaded not guilty on the grounds of psychiatric problems following that blow to his head, and was subsequently cleared of arson. These days he is a reformed man and won a recall to Zimbabwe's Test squad in 2014.

3) INDIA'S WORLD CUP EXIT

When it comes to cricket-induced hysteria there's nowhere quite like the subcontinent. Indian fans didn't respond well to being dumped out of the 2007 World Cup at the group stage. Riots ensued as they took to the streets in their thousands, burning effigies of their former heroes for shaming their country. The higher the pedestal, the harder the fall – and the previously adored MS Dhoni fell hard. Furious fans vented their anger on his house and young fans who had grown their hair to imitate their idol chopped off their locks in disgust. But for some distressed fans a haircut wasn't enough. Twenty-eight villages in Haryana decided that cricket was no longer for them and banned the sport entirely, while a West Bengali farmer was so distraught that he hanged himself at his Calcutta home.

2) BODYLINE

Questions raised in parliament, frantic late-night phone calls, a breakdown in relations between the UK and Australia, and scars that remained for generations – all over a few bumpers? When Jardine, Larwood and co. hatched the Bodyline tactic to counter Bradman in the 1932/33 Ashes, no one could have envisaged a controversy of such seismically silly proportions. A riot was narrowly averted in the third Test at Adelaide after Larwood struck Aussie skipper Bill Woodfull above the heart and smacked wicketkeeper Bert Oldfield on the head. Things got so out of perspective that England were ready to jump back on the boat and head home after accusations of unsporting behaviour from the Australian Cricket Board. A truce of sorts was eventually reached when Australia withdrew their complaints fearing the financial loss of a cancelled tour, but the bitterness and anger provoked by Bodyline lasted for generations.

1) HAIR IN THE HEADLIGHTS

It was an end-of-summer dead rubber in 2006, which seemed to be heading towards a pride-salvaging Pakistani win when, on the fourth afternoon, umpire Darrell Hair suddenly decided, on his own, that Pakistan had been illegally scuffing the ball. Instead of first having a quiet word in private, Hair showily accused Pakistan of foul play and declared mid-session that a five-run penalty be doled out. After the tea break, Inzamam's team refused to take the field and half an hour of crazed and fruitless diplomacy couldn't prevent the game being declared a forfeit, a Test cricket first. England were awarded the match, and everyone went home confused and disillusioned. The matter didn't end there. In response to the ICC reading out emails from Hair, in which he said he would resign in return for $500,000, the disgraced umpire completed his meltdown by taking his case to the High Court, claiming he had been a victim of racial discrimination. We're not kidding. ∎

Curtly Ambrose
and Steve
Waugh almost
came to blows
in Trinidad

Fights and Feuds

LET'S GET READY TO RUUUUUUMBLE

10) CURTLY AMBROSE V STEVE WAUGH

Shane Warne has called the confrontation between Steve Waugh and Curtly Ambrose "the worst incident I have seen on the field". In 1994/95, with West Indies 1-0 down against Australia and their grip on the long-held title of the world's best side slipping, Ambrose came out fighting at Port of Spain. With Australia's first innings crumbling, a typically obdurate knock from Waugh was frustrating Ambrose. After a series of explosive bouncers, Ambrose eyeballed Waugh. With Ambrose going for the silent-but-deadly treatment, Waugh posited the question: "Why don't you go and get f****d." Ambrose had to be dragged away and he responded with a five-fer as Australia were bowled out for 128. Ambrose later admitted that, "In the heat of the moment I really wanted to physically beat him."

9) GRAEME SMITH V HERSCHELLE GIBBS

Kevin Pietersen's infamous 2015 autobiography is pure Enid Blyton compared to that of South Africa's tearaway Herschelle Gibbs. Drinking binges, match-fixing, drug-taking and hotel orgies added 50 shades of black to the invariably sanitised world of sporting autobiographies. In the rare moments that he broke off to talk about cricket, Gibbs accused Graeme Smith of being too powerful

167

as captain, of effectively bullying coach Mickey Arthur and of forming cliques with the dominant personalities in the dressing-room. Smith shot back with: "I think it shows more about his own insecurities than anything else," and Gibbs never played for South Africa again.

8) RODNEY HOGG V KIM HUGHES

Former Aussie captain Kim Hughes had always attracted ill-feeling from teammates – including having dead animals dumped in his cricket bag at his first club – and the Australian dressing-room was brimming with mutiny in the early 1980s, led by macho heavyweights Dennis Lillee and Rod Marsh. Tensions reached a very public nadir at Port of Spain in 1984 when feisty fast bowler Rodney Hogg, steaming that Hughes wasn't giving him the field he wanted, threw a punch at his captain. A year later, both of their international careers ended ignobly but perhaps fittingly on the Australian rebel tour to South Africa in 1985.

7) SHANE WARNE V KEVIN PIETERSEN

Shane Warne and KP's friendship is combustible. It's all about ego: when not flattering each other's, they're attacking it. Warne even got the old pots and kettles out to dub Pietersen "the walking ego" but it was the Aussie who allowed his own to get the better of him at Brisbane in the first Test of the 2006/07 Ashes. With Australia finding wickets hard to come by in England's second innings, Warne's frustrations erupted and he threw the ball at Pietersen, who defended himself with his bat before calling Warne a "f**kwit". It may well be the most succinct thing KP has ever said.

6) INZAMAM-UL-HAQ V SHIV KUMAR THIND

When Indian cricket fan Shiv Kumar Thind started calling Inzamam-ul-Haq a "mota aloo" (fat potato) while he was fielding during an ODI in Toronto in 1997, he was asking for trouble. Especially as he was using a megaphone to air his views. Inzy finally snapped and, grabbing a bat that had suddenly and rather suspiciously appeared on the boundary, bulldozed into the stands, wielding his weapon. With the megaphone-warrior seconds from a mashing, security and spectators flocked in to restrain the great man.

5) SHANE WARNE V ARJUNA RANATUNGA

As insults go, it's certainly imaginative: "He's probably… swallowed a sheep or something". Shane Warne, who often looked as if he had had a bellyful of farmyard animals himself, was talking about his similarly rotund nemesis Arjuna Ranatunga. Their feud went back to Sri Lanka's tempestuous tour of Australia in 1995/96, when Muttiah Muralitharan was called for no-balling by Australian umpire Darrell Hair. A year later it escalated. With Sri Lanka closing in on a historic World Cup final victory, Warne was bowling at Ranatunga in the battle of the bulge. A flipper turned into a full toss and Ranatunga launched Warne into the stands. Since then, Ranatunga has called Warne overrated while Warne has returned the favour by saying Ranatunga is "without any question… the most difficult opponent I have come across". And by opponent, he means bastard.

4) HARBHAJAN SINGH V RICKY PONTING

Relations between Australia and India became as hostile as any we've seen in Test cricket during those testy, tasty rubbers of 2007/08 and 2008/09. It wasn't funny, it wasn't clever, and it certainly wasn't pretty. But it was compulsive viewing. And Australia's street-fighting skipper and India's supreme wind-up merchant were at the very heart of it. Their mutual antipathy dated back to 1998 and a day/nighter in Sharjah when a 17-year-old Harbhajan, playing in just his fourth ODI, had Ponting stumped. Harbhajan celebrated by marching down the wicket, shouting in his face and giving him some very specific directions back to the pavilion. Ponting responded with a volley of his own and a shoulder barge, vowing that he would one day have revenge.

The problem for Ponting was that it never really worked out that way, at least not from a personal perspective. Harbhajan dismissed Ponting on ten occasions in Tests – more than any other bowler – including three ducks. It was no great surprise that when Harbhajan picked up his 300th Test victim, Ponting was that man. Of course, unassuming fellow that he is, Harbhajan didn't like to make a big deal out of it. "Ponting has a lot to say about our players and about the way we play our cricket," he said in 2009. "In fact, it is Ponting who first needs to go and learn to bat against spin bowling. I can get Ponting out any time."

3) DON BRADMAN V BILL O'REILLY

Bill O'Reilly, the greatest Australian spinner never to have gone out with Liz Hurley, was apparently never shy of telling people that the Don Bradman Appreciation Society would fit inside a telephone box. (A note to kids: a telephone box was once used to make telephone calls in prehistoric times before mobile phones.) The great Australian side of the 1930s and '40s was, O'Reilly claimed, often divided on sectarian grounds between the Catholics and the rest. A strict Protestant, Bradman was respected – how could you not respect a man with an average hovering around 100 – but rarely liked by his teammates, and he held a long-lasting grudge against O'Reilly. "You could say we did not like each other, but it would be closer to the truth to say we chose to have little to do with each other," O'Reilly wrote in his autobiography. "Bradman was a teetotaller, ambitious, conservative and meticulous. I was outspoken and gregarious, an equally ambitious young man of Irish descent."

2) DENNIS LILLEE V JAVED MIANDAD

In the early 1980s, Javed Miandad and Dennis Lillee were box office. In the first Test of Pakistan's 1981/82 tour of Australia, the visitors had been set an improbable 543 for victory. Miandad came in at 27 for 2 with Lillee in full nostril-flaring mode. As Miandad ambled for a single, Lillee deliberately stepped across his path and was shoved out of the way before following him down the pitch and landing a side-footed kick to the batsman's thigh. Miandad raised his bat like an executioner, Lillee raised his fists like a Victorian boxer, and umpire Tony Crafter had to separate them before a bit of Tom and Jerry could turn full Tarantino.

1) IAN BOTHAM V IAN CHAPPELL

Between them, Ian Botham and Ian Chappell have played 177 Tests, scored 10,545 Tests runs, competed in 15 Ashes series, spent 129 years on Earth and sported some truly magnificent furry critters above their top lips. So you would think they might have something in common to talk about. Instead, 37 years after they allegedly first came to blows in a bar-room brawl at the MCG, the moustaches may have gone but the flames of animosity show no sign of burning out. Like a cricketing Stalin v Trotsky (or Blur v Oasis, depending on how you like your cultural references), Chappell and Botham have spent the last four decades sniping, fighting, accusing and denying. Chappell says that Botham is "peddling lies and fairy-tales"; Botham says Chappell "worries me about as much as a cold". Both men are grandfathers. ■

WEBCO
SINCE 1905 **TOOLS**

WE BURY SHEEP THROUGH QUALITY, STRENGTH AND ORIGINALITY

SA's #1 Hand Tool Brand

Telephone: +27 11 452 5906
Fax Line: +27 11 452 3548
Email Address: sales@webcotools.co.za

Jacques Kallis was the face of
one of South Africa's more
bizarre advertisement campaigns

Brazen Product Endorsements

FROM PORN AND PATE LACQUER TO
RABBIT-KILLER AND RUM

10) "ROD MARSH SAYS *PARADE* MAGAZINE IS A MAN'S BEST BUY"

Back in the Seventies, a naff *Nuts*-prototype that had been comforting lonely British men for decades discovered a few more readers in Australia, and got Rod Marsh to front their ad campaign. A legendary tinnie-crusher and professional Australian, Marsh was *Parade* magazine's obvious choice to tap into the Aussie men's market. In Christian Ryan's book *Golden Boy: Kim Hughes and the bad old days of Australian cricket*, the writer recalls Marsh's "Baggy Green and larrikin smirk cresting the latest month's busty covergirl", accompanied by a few lines about *king hugh and his amazing sex secrets*. Different times...

9) "IT'S MY RUM OF CHOICE, EVERY TIME" – SIR GARFIELD SOBERS

"Sir Garry". The name alone conjures up many memories: 8,000 Test runs, 26 centuries, 235 wickets, six sixes in an over, 365 not out, and a bottle of Cockspur rum. Indeed, to mark Sobers' achievements, the good people at Cockspur decided to honour him with his very own 2004 vintage: "Yours to savour and enjoy", and complete with authentic Sir Garfield signature on every bottle. Cockspur VSOR has won awards for quality and acclaim from connoisseurs across the globe, including Sir Garfield himself.

8) "WE BURY SHEEP" – JACQUES KALLIS

A mysterious work of brilliant dada weirdness, this surreal slab of comedy first appeared in a South African cricket magazine, and boy is it strange. There's Jacques Kallis, mid-pose, clasping his new Webco spade, and readying himself for what can only be some after-hours sheep-burying. And how exactly is Jacques preparing to bury these woolly impostors? Why, with quality, strength and originality of course! How else would an international all-rounder bury his sheep?

7) "NOT OUT! AND I'VE BEEN SMOKING THIS PIPE OF ST BRUNO FLAKE FOR THE BEST PART OF AN HOUR" – JOHN ARLOTT

It's not just players who have fallen in with the world of advertising. John Arlott, a greatly respected writer and the finest commentator of his era, rose to prominence more through luck than judgment, as he himself admitted. But his dark Hampshire burr and languid delivery made him the ideal figure to evoke the otherworldly majesty of "rolling your own". In John's case, it was only natural that his pipe would be filled with St Bruno. "The most popular flake of all," said the voice of summer, a wordsmith who would often leave his colleagues wondering how he thought up his poetic phrases. This one was probably dreamt up in a smoke-filled ad exec's office.

6) "MMMMMMM… KFC"

Cricket has never quite taken off with our cousins across the Atlantic, but one brand tried its best to bring a little culture to the masses with KFC's "Cricket Survival Guide". The ads used players like Michael Clarke and Mitchell Johnson to promote their "Backyard Bucket". But after allegations of racism from American viewers directed at one particular clip of a white Aussie supporter placating a crowd of black West Indian supporters with some fried chicken, the ads were pulled. Probably for the best.

5) "NONE OF MY CRICKETING FOES CAUSED ANYWHERE NEAR AS MUCH DAMAGE AS WHAT THE RABBIT HAS INFLICTED ON AUSTRALIAN SOIL" – GLENN MCGRATH

The former Aussie seamer put his name to a product very close to his sheep-farmer's heart – a strain of virus aimed at killing those evil bunnies who abuse the Australian soil. Widely regarded as a rabbit with the bat, it seems compassion for his fellow furry friends isn't one of McGrath's strong points.

4) "ALL THOSE FOR THE SHREDDED WHEAT TOUR, FOLLOW ME" – IAN BOTHAM

Now here's an offer! Join Botham in the role of Willy Wonka, taking the world's cereal-lovers on a tour *inside* a giant, fabled Shredded Wheat! Roll up, roll up! This came at the end of three decades' work as the frontman of the no-nonsense cereal, a beautiful relationship predicated on Botham's superhuman ability to put away three of those wheaty bad boys, leaving us withered mortals at home in our dressing gowns eaten up with inadequacy as we force-feed ourselves a measly second.

3) "IT'S AMAZING WHERE GOOD HAIR GETS YOU" – KEVIN PIETERSEN

A "confident swagger and creative style" may make you a target on and off the pitch, but for Kevin Pietersen it has delivered some rather tasty commercial offshoots. Revealed as the new Brylcreem Boy in 2009, taking over the lacquer from the original dasher, Denis

Compton, KP took to his new role with gusto, but admitted he had "big shoes to fill" after becoming the first celebrity to front the hair gel since David Beckham was dropped in 1999 for shaving his golden head. The adverts were spectacularly smug, with our hero leaning back with his feet up on the president's White House desk as a dumbstruck "Obama" looks on from the side.

2) "I CAN PLAY CRICKET, SWIM OR DO WHATEVER I WANT!" – GRAHAM GOOCH

The godless world of barnet regrowth remains cricket's favourite advertising opportunity. As daily cap-wearers, these days cricket's masses are almost exclusively bald (don't be fooled – they're all wearing syrups), and this fact, accentuated by the slap-head pates of depressed under-performing batsmen, can have devastating effects on team morale. Thankfully help is at hand from the Advanced Hair Studio, who profess to have helped restore the regal locks of, amongst others, Shane Warne, Graham Gooch and Michael Vaughan.

1) "COLMAN'S MUSTARD, LIKE GRACE, HEADS THE FIELD"

Commercialism is by no means a new phenomenon. In 1895, WG Grace became the first sportsman to cross from sports-product advertising into the general product market when he became the face of Colman's mustard. Colman's produced a stunning, and stunningly timeless, full-colour advertisement in which the Good Doctor strides forth from the pavilion accompanied by the tagline "Colman's Mustard Heads the Field". An early-day Beckham in recognisability and stature, the choice of product seemed to suit the great Victorian's character quite well: a spicy, confrontational individual who wasn't afraid to bend the rules. ■

Heavy Grubbers

THE HISTORY OF THE GAME IS FULL OF CURIOUS CULINARY YARNS

10) ROD MARSH'S MALT SANDWICHES

Sandwiches lie at the heart of the cricket-playing experience, and most of us consider the tastiness of the interval sarnies a crucial part of the whole show. But not so, apparently, for grizzled Aussie legend Rod Marsh. The culture of drinking in Australian cricket in the Chappell–Lillee era is said to have been formidable, and Marsh was, according to teammates, not only prolific behind the stumps. When reminded, late of an evening after play that he hadn't eaten since the tea break, Marsh would reply: "I've had 20 malt sandwiches." Better than cucumber, sure, but not a patch on cheese and pickle.

9) WARNE SERVES UP VARIATION

As English batsmen made hay during the 2010/11 Ashes, and successive baggy-greened spin bowlers fell by the wayside, the hosts must have felt like calling for the help of Shane Warne. The pre-transformation retiree did his best to distract his old mate Kevin Pietersen as he approached a double-hundred in Adelaide. With Doug Bollinger entering delivery stride, KP suddenly – and annoyingly for a bowler for whom running to the wicket is no formality – pulled away.

The reason? Shane Warne's face was plastered over the sightscreen next to a McDonald's chicken burger, much to the amusement of the legendary twirler's Sky commentary colleagues.

8) GAFFER'S GRILLED CHICKEN

Touring the subcontinent can be a difficult business, and many a cricketer has spent a day's play MIA while nursing a viral complaint in their hotel room. But some go to extreme lengths to avoid discomfort. Alec Stewart famously ate the Presbyterian meal of skinless grilled chicken and sauce-less vegetables for 40 consecutive nights on tour in India. His teammate of 12 years Mike Atherton, who was keener to sample the exotic – though more dangerous – local dishes on offer, wrote in his autobiography that Stewart "has a narrow focus on sport and life" and added: "I often wonder whether he will look back with regret at some of the missed opportunities touring life offers." Mind you, the Gaffer played for England until he was 40, so we guess he was doing something right.

7) TRES GOES BANG

Marcus Trescothick's love affair with the sausage is well known. Nicknamed "Banger" to this day, as a child his affection for the porky articles was passionate and profound. "Sausages were my favourite," he wrote in his autobiography, before describing his schoolboy diet thus: "sausages, chips, sausages, toast, sausages, baked beans, sausages, cheese, sausages, eggs, sausages and the occasional sausage thrown in, topped off with a sprinkling of sausage." Not recommended by today's nutritionists, but a sportsman needs his protein.

6) THE BIG BUCKET BIG BASH

The Australia team used to appear in adverts for healthy breakfast cereal Weet-Bix, but these days it's KFC who are all over Aussie cricket like a tasty breadcrumb coating on a leg of greasy bird. Channel 9's coverage of the Big Bash League has the commentators singing the Colonel's praises during play, and has offered to reward the winner of the KFC Classic Catches Competition with "a year's supply of KFC". Stuart MacGill once refused to appear in a KFC advert as part of his Cricket Australia contract, pointing to hypocrisy after he was told by the management that he needed to lose weight. "Cricket Australia and KFC would say they're promoting a healthy lifestyle," he said, "but it's tripe." Not strictly true, Stu, but we get where you're coming from.

5) RAVI FEATHERS HIS NEST

Talking of chicken, another man partial to the fried variety is none other than Ravi Bopara. The Essex batsman owns two fried chicken shops in London; a smallish one down in Tooting and the mothership in East Ham which is run by his brother, cousin and father. Ravi, who's a regular visitor to his Sam's Chicken shops, isn't resting on his laurels and is looking at other opportunities in the restaurant world. "I don't want to stick my eggs all in one basket," he says, which seems a fitting mantra for a chicken-shop owner.

4) GOUGHY'S COOKERY SCHOOL

Ever the modern man, in 2010 Darren Gough launched an online cookery school for men in the run-up to Christmas called *Give The Bird A Break*, which, he assured us at the time, "is a great name". He explained: "What I've done is show men how easy it is to cook good meat and give the other half a break. While they're out shopping and doing the wrapping we should be in the kitchen with a pinny on." Dazzling stuff.

3) THE RUSSELL DIET

Former England and Gloucestershire keeper Jack Russell was an oddity in a number of ways, particularly his eating habits. His lunch on match days consisted of two Weetabix soaked in milk for exactly 12 minutes (he got the twelfth man to pour the milk eight minutes before he came off the field). Teammates say he drank upwards of 20 cups of tea over the course of a Test match, using the same tea bag, which he would hang on a nail in the dressing-room between brews. Although Russell's favourite dinner was mashed potato, baked beans and HP sauce, Angus Fraser recalls that, on the 1994/95 tour to Australia, the bushy-lipped gloveman went to the same Chinese restaurant every evening and asked for "chicken and cashew nuts", with the small amendment that the cashew nuts be taken out. Fruit cake, anyone?

2) BOBBIE'S BUFFET

The India–Pakistan rivalry has produced plenty of victims over the years, but in the run-up to the nations' cricket teams meeting in the 2011 World Cup, there were two unlikely beneficiaries. Assistant sub-inspector Rakesh Rasella and sub-inspector Ramphal of the Chandigarh police enjoyed three lavish meals a day at the luxury Taj Hotel in Chandigarh to check for poisoning, in case of sabotage of the players' preparations. Rasella told the *Times of India*: "I have tasted more than 18 different dishes before they were consumed by cricketers and I hadn't eaten many of them ever [before]."

1) AT HOME WITH BEEFY AND LAMBY

As meatily built as they were meatily named (or nicknamed), Ian Botham and Allan Lamb's long-haired, mustachioed cartoon faces filled our TV screens when they starred in those ads for quality-assured meat a few years ago. In one, with Lamb cooking a leg of, well, lamb, Botham polished a red onion on his trousers before adding it to the roasting tray. Not comedy gold, but let's face it, the cartoon Beefy and Lamby knocking around their shared fictional home – in full whites and pads – indulging in repartee over a roast dinner, while Blowers does the voiceover... You can't buy that kind of magic. ■

Lalit Modi at London's
High Court in 2012

Legal Battles

SOME OF CRICKET'S MESSIEST AND MOST LURID BATTLES HAVE REQUIRED MORE THAN THE JUDGMENT OF AN UMPIRE TO SETTLE MATTERS

10) PARVISH LAND WRANGLE, 1598

Pinpointing the exact age of cricket is trickier than pinpointing the exact age of Shahid Afridi. What's more certain, however, is that the first known reference to the game came during a 16th-century Surrey legal dispute when an area of scrubland was appropriated by one John Parvish in order to establish a timber yard. In the subsequent ownership battle, a written deposition about the area was made by a local coroner John Derrick in which he attested that, "Being a scholler in the ffree schoole of Guldeford, hee and diverse of his fellows did runne and play there at creckett and other plaies". Derrick was 59 at the time, thus dating cricket's known recorded history back to at least the 1550s.

9) REED V SEYMOUR, 1927

The modern cricketer undoubtedly has greater post-retirement options available to him than his predecessors, but not every player has the quickstep of Mark Ramprakash or Phil Tufnell's taste for the more exotic parts of a kangaroo's anatomy. As such, the benefit match – or rather the benefit year as it has become – offers a vital boost to the coffers of retiring players who, thanks to Kent's James Seymour, enjoy their pension supplement tax free (at least until the new legislation kicked in in April 2017). After being granted a benefit match in 1920, the county stalwart fought against the revenue's claims upon his financial "gift" and seven years later the House of Lords eventually ruled in his favour. Sadly Seymour didn't get to enjoy the extra money for long. He died just three years later, aged 50.

8) MILLER V JACKSON, 1977

There can be few village cricketers who haven't had to sheepishly retrieve the ball from a nearby private garden at one time or another under the tutting gaze of the homeowner. In the 1970s, however, Lintz Cricket Club's ground was effectively shut down after its neighbours, the Millers, tired of sixes whizzing into their garden and successfully sought an injunction banning play. The ramifications for local clubs throughout Britain were huge, but thankfully the House of Lords again came to cricket's rescue by overturning the original decision, ruling that financial compensation for any individual bit of property damage was sufficient remedy. In his judgment, Lord Denning remarked, "In summertime, village cricket is the delight of everyone". Everyone, that is, except the Millers.

7) GREIG V INSOLE, 1978

The seeds of the modern franchise tournament can be traced back to the glitz of Kerry Packer's World Series Cricket. Former England captain Tony Greig was recruited as its poster boy, but English cricket's governing body took a dim view of snazzy overseas competitions that caught the eye of their players. The ECB's forerunner, the TCCB, banned anyone who was set to play in the event from returning to recognised first-class cricket – a prescriptive move also supported by the ICC. After a marathon 32-day case, Greig had the ban overturned in the British High Court, a decision which still now allows Bollywood actors to waste troves of money recruiting middling international imports to their IPL sides.

6) BOTHAM AND LAMB V KHAN, 1996

After Mike Gatting's famously pointed row with umpire Shakoor Rana in 1987 and the ball-tampering allegations of the 1992 "Wasim and Waqar tour", relations between English and Pakistani cricket were towards the snowman end of frosty. Matters worsened still further when Pakistan's skipper Imran Khan apparently wrote a couple of magazine articles accusing Ian Botham and Allan Lamb of some seam-rearranging of their own, as well as suggesting they were "racist, ill-educated and lacking in class". The pair sued for libel, but the judge accepted Khan had been misinterpreted, leaving the England stars with a huge legal bill.

5) JUSTICE QAYYUM'S ENQUIRY, 2000

The Hansie Cronje spiral of shame was already starting to unravel in 2000, but the cricketers with the dubious distinction of being the first ever to be officially found guilty of match-fixing were Pakistan internationals Salim Malik and Ata-ur-Rehman. After a year-long enquiry, the pair were banned from the game for life by Justice Qayyum in a judgment in which he also cleared Wasim Akram and Mushtaq Ahmed, but rather coyly recommended they never be allowed to captain the national side in future, saying the former "cannot be said to be above suspicion".

4) ATHERTON V ASGHAR ALI, 2000

After notching a duck in a heavy defeat to South Africa at the 1996 World Cup, England's captain was unable to understand a question from Pakistani journalist Asghar Ali at the post-match press conference. Having asked for the query to be repeated twice with no further inroads into comprehension made, Athers misguidedly scoffed, "Can someone get this buffoon out of here?" When Atherton arrived in Karachi in 2000 for England's tour of Pakistan, Ali was there waiting for him, claiming he would sue unless he received a written apology for the slight which he alleged had ruined his professional life and cost him his fiancée because she didn't want to marry a "buffoon". Ali was actually granted a court date in Islamabad, but the matter was settled when the ECB issued an apology on Atherton's behalf.

3) DEUTSCHER HANDBALLBUND EV V MAROS KOLPAK, 2003

EU workers cannot be discriminated against on the grounds of nationality in another member state, but Kolpak was a Slovakian who fell foul of the "two foreigners" rule in operation in German handball because at the time his country was not a full EU member. Slovakia only had a trade "association agreement" with Brussels, which meant Kolpak's club had to use him as an overseas player and he subsequently lost his contract. He challenged the classification, and the European Court of Justice ruled that an association agreement alone was enough to confer EU status on a player from such a country. As Brussels had similar arrangements with countries including South Africa, Jamaica and Zimbabwe, this meant cricketers from those countries could be labelled as non-overseas, and so circumvent overseas quotas in county cricket. The rules have since been tightened and ECB financial incentives for fielding homegrown players increased, but the decision still largely holds.

2) CAIRNS V MODI, 2012

Foxes with bits of chicken feather stuck between their teeth arouse less suspicion than the ill-fated Indian Cricket League did during its brief existence. Marred by bizarre collapses and comical run-outs, Kiwi all-rounder Chris Cairns took part in the tournament and was later accused on Twitter by Lalit Modi – proud father of the ICL's officially sanctioned rival, the IPL – of being involved in match-fixing during his stint with the Chandigarh Lions. The judge ruled in Cairns' favour and ordered Modi to pay damages of £90,000 and costs of £1.5m. Cairns said after the ruling that, "I can once again walk into any cricket ground in the world with my head held high." Cairns was later accused of lying under oath during the trial but was found not guilty of perjury and attempting to pervert the course of justice in a second trial in 2015.

1) INDIAN SUPREME COURT V SRINIVASAN, 2014

Despite the 2013 IPL betting scandal involving both his own son-in-law and the Chennai Super Kings franchise, former BCCI president N Srinivasan clung on to power like a limpet throughout the investigations that followed. He then attempted to appoint his own panel to look into the affair, a move rejected by the Indian Supreme Court, who ordered that he finally quit his post. In an unsavoury twist, Srinivasan was appointed as the first chairman of the revamped ICC in 2014, with newly enhanced responsibility for cleaning up corruption in the global game. Mercifully the BCCI finally saw sense and unanimously voted to stand him down from the job a year later. ∎

Billy Bowden gives
Glenn McGrath his
marching orders

Send-Offs

THERE'S NOTHING MORE DELICIOUSLY NAFF
AND BORDERLINE APPALLING THAN A
WELL-STAGED SEND-OFF

10) MARLON'S SALUTE

The Samuels/Stokes will-they-won't-they affair added a certain Bogart/Bacall shimmer to the 2015 West Indies–England Test series. They had been at each other for days, until in the dusk of an early Grenadian evening, Stokes bunted a rank long-hop straight to deep mid-wicket. As Stokes dragged himself off, Samuels stood alone, waiting for his man to pass. And as he did, Samuels bowed his head, a serviceman by a graveside, and clasped his sunhat close to his chest. As his fallen soldier passed, Samuels raised his right hand in sombre salute. Stokes, bless him, called him a c**t. And they say love is dead.

9) ROD'S THUMB

"Rod Tucker". Stage name, right? Like "Chopper Reid" and "Dame Edna"? Must be. He's meant to be an umpire, but he's really a lab-produced Australian essence congealed into human form, never better exemplified than when Tucker squints down the pitch at the snivelling little weed at the other end and gives him the "on yer bike" thumb gesture when the finger's not quite enough. It's got a Gene Hackman quality to it – our sheriff throwing open the saloon doors and, with one thumb movement, ridding the bar of unwanted failures. When the umpire sends you off with a sneer, you have to wonder for cricket's soul.

8) TICKETS, PLEASE!

Merv Hughes, bushy of 'tache and generous of girth, was bowling at Javed Miandad, similarly bushy and girthy. Despite appearances, it wasn't exactly a meeting of minds. Hughes – who valued sledging as highly as he did his subscription to *Retro Facial Hair Monthly* – was told by Mr Miandad that he was nothing but a fat bus conductor. Harsh, but half right. Just a few deliveries later Miandad was dismissed by Hughes – presumably because he wasn't carrying his railcard – and "Ding, ding, tickets please!" roared a very happy Aussie bowler. An oldie but a goodie.

7) ABSOLUTELY BATTY

County cricket: the preserve of the slow, the quiet, the antiquated; home to ladies' pavilions, cake-lovers, deckchair owners and floppy-hat wearers. Not so when Gareth "really angry" Batty is around. 2013 saw Surrey meet Somerset in a T20 quarter-final, with Batty bowling, all bouncy run-up and energetic action. Peter Trego – tattoo-sleeved and bulky – went for the reverse-sweep and was bowled. Normal, everyday stuff. That is, until Batty went totally crazy. He screamed, he swore, he postured. Trego walked towards him – it was the way off – and, while it wasn't quite ice hockey, it practically all kicked off. Punches weren't thrown but it looked like they were considered. Batty was banned for two games and we were all left to wonder why he was so furious.

6) SILLY BILLY

Australians are good at many things. Surfing, sport, surfing – they're inevitably the life and soul of the hostel. But arguably one thing the Brits have got over them is a sense of humour. Sure, Aussies can be funny, but there's a weird relationship between blokiness and being Australian that doesn't appear to lend itself to Brits' obviously hilarious self-effacing ways. Cue the first ever T20 international and a different kind of send-off. It was Australia v New Zealand, Billy "the personality" Bowden was umpiring, and the game was in the bag for the Aussies. For the penultimate ball Glenn McGrath pretended – he was pretending, you see – to bowl an underarm delivery, mimicking Trevor Chappell in 1981. Billy was all over it, red card out, contorting his body like a drunk Andy Serkis, cavorting and performing to the crowd. Its unfunniness will have you in hysterics.

5) AAMIR BLIP

Aamir Sohail: a languid left-hander from Lahore, with a temper to burn barns. Venkatesh Prasad: a gentle giant by pace-bowling standards, but buoyed by an electric Bangalore crowd (his home) in the 1996 World Cup quarter-final. A barney was in the offing. With Sohail going great guns on 55, he skipped down and carved Prasad to the boundary, before wagging his finger at the bowler and pointing to the ball, which had shot through extra-cover. Prasad, continuing around the wicket, cramped Sohail for room as he attempted a similar shot, and took out his off stump. Prasad told him where to go ("home") while questioning the nature of his parentage – as India went on to win by 39.

4) JIMMY SHOOSH

Remember that winter, when everything just worked? When the batsmen made the runs, the bowlers took the wickets, Steve Smith was rubbish, Clarke and Punter couldn't buy a run and Mitch Johnson was more Village People than Village of the Damned? It was England's time. Mitch was desperately trying to keep face, and failing. "Why you chirping now, mate? Not getting any wickets?" he blustered, as Anderson walked back to his mark. Next ball, Jimmy cleaned up Ryan Harris and turned in his follow-through to Mitch at the non-striker's, giving him the full "Jim The Redeemer" pose followed by the footballer's favourite – the "finger on the lips" effort. It wasn't big, clever or witty in any conceivable way. But it was still great.

3) PIGEON COO

"That's the first one!" cooed Glenn McGrath as he saw off Andrew Strauss at Bristol. The 2005 ODI Tri-series involving England,

Australia and Bangladesh was as much a part of the summer's narrative as Blair's back garden or the Edgbaston practice ball – and Pidge knew it would be so. So when he had England's opener bowled early on in the second game of the summer (following the T20 at the Rose Bowl), he waved him goodbye with a reminder: there's plenty more where that came from. As it happened, Strauss would make two centuries in the subsequent Ashes series (the only bloke to do so) and the match at Bristol? That was turned by a 65-ball 91 not-out from some young punk with a streak of blue in his hair.

2) WARNE ROCKS HUDSON

It was Australia's first trip to South Africa since their readmission, and it was all a bit much for Warne. During the first Test (in Johannesburg in 1994), having bowled Andrew Hudson round his legs, the young Shane charged towards him – adrenalin coursing through his ample cheeks – screaming: "F*** off. Go on, Hudson, f*** off out of here!" Even the Aussies hadn't seen anything like it before. Ian Healy – ever the friendly mediator – restrained him. According to *Wisden*, "Rarely on a cricket field has physical violence seemed so close."

1) SHARMA'S HAPPY SLAPPING

It was the deciding game of a closely fought series. In the first Test, Dinesh Chandimal's career-defining 162 not out had given Sri Lanka the most unlikely of victories, making him India's most-prized wicket. And he and Ishant Sharma had beef, having almost come to blows, bizarrely enough, because the Indian seamer had smiled at Dhammika Prasad after avoiding a short ball. But although all this made the fast bowler's decision to give Chandimal a send-off after dismissing him in the fourth innings understandable, it did nothing to explain the nature of the celebration itself. Ishant repeatedly slapped himself vigorously on the forehead while simultaneously head-banging, as if he had a bee trapped in his wild locks. A weird reaction, but fitting from one of international cricket's most endearingly eccentric characters. ∎

The Downright Weird

> "I UNDERSTAND CRICKET – WHAT'S GOING ON, THE SCORING – BUT I CAN'T UNDERSTAND WHY"
>
> BILL BRYSON

And so to the business end, and the section some, none, or all of you came here looking for. It barely needs stating that cricket's relationship with weirdness goes way beyond the bounds of common decency, into strange and peculiar netherworlds of hoaxers and impostors, blaggers, liggers and fibbers, fictitious cricketers, iffy nicknames, dodgy fashion statements, and cheese. Lots and lots of cheese. This is the stuff that elevates cricket, the game of gods and kings, to an even higher state of consciousness. After all, as the great Keith Miller says: "I've seen batting all over the world. And in other countries too."

Unlikeliest Fans

FROM POLITICIANS TO POP POETS

10) MARTIN MCGUINNESS

Never has a man nor a name so embodied the Irish Republic, yet the Sinn Fein stalwart and deputy first minister has made no secret of his love of England's national sport. It helps when you can brag about Kevin O'Brien's exploits against England in the 2011 World Cup (McGuiness lauded the all-rounder as a national hero), but in truth he fell in love with the game in the late Sixties and publically hailed England's 2005 Ashes victory.

9) CHRISTIAN VIERI

The Italian footballing legend is a usually quiet man but there was not a moment's hesitation when, in a press conference, he was asked which player he idolised as a boy. "Allan Border," he said. "Allan who?" replied the press corps. "Who did he play for?" "Australia," said Vieri. "At cricket." They were none the wiser. Vieri grew up in Sydney and could have made a fine professional cricketer if his Italian father Roberto had not decided to move the family home to Bologna after a decade in Australia.

8) ROGER FEDERER

If a bomb had gone off at Wimbledon on Saturday 25 June 2011, not only would the whole of south-west London have been treated to a shower of overpriced strawberries and cream, but two of the world's most naturally gifted sportsmen would have also been obliterated in one cruel explosion. Following another routine win at SW19, Roger Federer met up with Sachin Tendulkar – who had been watching Federer's match with his wife – to indulge in the sort of mutual back-slapping that would be interminable if they both weren't such thoroughly nice blokes. Later on Twitter, Tendulkar wrote that Federer was a "humble guy" who knew a lot about cricket.

7) THE TALIBAN

The Taliban aren't exactly known for yo-yoing but, having rejected cricket out of hand, the Afghanistan cricket team's increasingly impressive performances on the world stage were enough to capture the imagination of even the Islamic fundamentalists. During a Q&A posted on their official website, one user asked for the Taliban's stance on cricket. They responded: "We support all those sports that are good for health and have a noble purpose. You and other sports fans should be made aware of that fact that cricket was made official by the Taliban when they were in power." Ahead of 2012's historic ODI between Afghanistan and Pakistan, a spokesman for the Taliban also contacted the Afghanistan Cricket Board to wish the team well. How sweet.

6) KIRSTEN DUNST

It's not often that a Hollywood glamourpuss rocks up to a May Test match, but that's what we got in 2007 when Kirsten Dunst (*Spiderman, Melancholia,* etc) found herself watching Paul Collingwood edge his way to a century against West Indies at Lord's. Whether it was Colly's scratchy search for runs or the incessant posturing of her boyfriend, the Razorlight lead poseur Johnny Borrell, she hasn't been seen at HQ since, and she chucked the cricket-mad Borrell just weeks after seeing Colly turn it on. Coincidence? We'll let you decide.

5) DIETMAR HAMANN

A footballer and a German one at that, Hamann developed an unlikely love for cricket during the 2005 Ashes and once turned out for Alderley Edge CC second XI in the Cheshire County Cricket League. In his 2012 autobiography, Hamann admitted to alcohol and gambling addictions following his departure from Liverpool in 2006, culminating in a loss of £288,400 while spread-betting during an Australia v South Africa Test. "That night I bought Australia for £2,800 at 340 runs. That meant for every run over 340 you win £2,800, but for every run under you lose the same amount," Hamann explained. "Australia collapsed for 237. It is a score I remember well. It cost me £288,400. Every wicket felt like a stab in the heart."

4) ADOLF HITLER

Introduced to the game as a POW during the Great War, the questionable theorist and all-round hoodlum believed he could use cricket to prepare his troops for battle... but not before he'd made a few key adjustments. Handshakes and encouraging taps on the bum weren't Adolf's bag, you see. And as for pads, these artificial "bolsters" were just downright unmanly. A bigger and harder ball was also on Hitler's list of "improvements", which may explain Germany's impressive record in Olympic shot put. Despite Hitler's reservations, he challenged the British to a friendly match in 1930, but had soon written the sport off as "insufficiently violent" for German fascists. In case you're wondering, it was intended as a criticism.

3) BARACK OBAMA

It stands to reason that the world's only true superhero would like his cricket. It began in 2009 with a few technical tips from Brian Lara during a trip to Trinidad ("I always wanted to meet the Michael Jordan of cricket"), and was cemented in a conversation with Dave Cameron when the two leaders met at the White House. After enduring a basketball game the previous evening, Cameron promised to teach Obama the intricacies of cricket and to take him to a game in England. Obama agreed, before a wag from the British press corps piped up: "Mr President, this is great you've agreed to learn about cricket. I notice the prime minister neglected to tell you that a Test match usually takes five days. So it's going to be a long trip." But what could be better than the leader of the free world plotting his next move from the Lord's pavilion?

2) MIKE SKINNER

Mike Skinner, beat-poet doyen of the post-club comedown whose band The Streets illuminated the tower blocks and stairwells of urban Britain in the Noughties, was always an unlikely cricket fan. Yet, as a dedicated chronicler of Englishness, he always had a soft spot for the game, even once referencing cricket in a song called "Addicted" about the perils of wasting your life in the bookies. So when England overcame Australia in 2010/11, Skinner was moved to commemorate the moment with his own spoken-word tribute. The day after victory at Sydney nailed a 3-1 win, a short video called *An English Corner* appeared on The Streets' website, featuring Skinner's dreamlike rendition of a passage from the last-day report from the *Guardian*'s Mike Selvey.

1) HUGH CORNWELL

One of punk's original gloom merchants, Cornwell has survived various dust-ups, run-ins and even a six-week stint at Pentonville to indulge his love of music and cricket. The bile and sneer evident in Stranglers songs like "Peaches" and "No More Heroes" may have been the marks of a natural agitator, but while his mates on the Old Kent Road were tearing down the establishment, Cornwell was cultivating a delicate passion for the game of kings. It all began with his father, who would listen to *Test Match Special* when Hugh was a boy, and when he learned that Fred Titmus had gone to his school, that was it. A lifetime in love with the game culminated in his own appearance on *TMS*'s "View From the Boundary". ∎

Brian Lara
introduced Barack
Obama to cricket

British actors Basil Radford and Naunton Wayne recreated a cricket scene from *The Pickwick Papers* at Rochester Festival in 1951

Fictional Characters

FROM PAGE AND SCREEN

10) QUANKO SAMBA
The Pickwick Papers (1836, Charles Dickens)

Dickens might be remembered for documenting the industrial filth and misery of 19th-century London, but he was a funny, funny man. And he wrote about cricket. In *The Pickwick Papers,* an unknown drunken spectator watching a match between All-Muggleton and Dingley Dell recalled the ill-fated heroism of a West Indian he knew called Quanko Samba: "'Iwentin; keptin-heat intense – natives all fainted – taken away – fresh half-dozen ordered – fainted also – Blazo bowling – supported by two natives – couldn't bowl me out – fainted too – cleared away the colonel – wouldn't give in – faithful attendant – Quanko Samba – last man left – sun so hot, bat in blisters, ball scorched brown – five hundred and seventy runs – rather exhausted – Quanko mustered up last remaining strength – bowled me out – had a bath, and went out to dinner...'" And bowlers reckon they put the yards in nowadays...

9) NEVILLE GRIBLEY
More Tales From a Long Room (1982, Peter Tinniswood)

From the fevered mind of Peter Tinniswood, Gribley is a hilarious parody of Ian Botham. A greengrocer by day, Gribley (also referred to as "Batman of Botham City" by the author) is "five foot three in his stocking feet, seven and a half stone... and a man of profound meekness, sensitivity and modesty", only revealing his extraordinary all-round abilities when he leaps into his blood-red Botham-mobile. In Tinniswood's surreal portrayal of a cricket-lover's Middle England, Botham is also the true identity of a multiplicity of celebrities, historical figures and politicians, including Hitler, the Duke of Wellington and Roy Hattersley, but it is Gribley – a man who spends his evenings relaxing with a "pot of Mazawattee tea and custard creams" – who is the silliest and funniest of Tinniswood's Bothams.

8) SAM PALMER
The Final Test (1953, dir. Anthony Asquith)

In this unapologetic slab of schmaltz, the story centres on the relationship between the ruddy, seen-better-days England batsman Sam Palmer, and his haughty, bookish son, Reggie. Sam's about to play in his last Test for England, and his strained efforts to persuade his boy to see him off at The Oval gathers pace and pathos as we build to the climax. It is a sentimental study of father–son relationships, with real-life cameos by England players of the day, who potter about in the background, smoking pipes, raffishly flicking through newspapers and uttering words of encouragement to outgoing batsmen. England skipper Len Hutton's wonderfully clipped Queen's English – straight out of Pudsey – is a comic joy, as is Denis Compton's semi-corpsing smirk from the back of the dressing-room.

7) PRADEEP MATHEW
Chinaman (2011, Shehan Karunatilaka)

This Tamil mystery-spinner's character is revealed, unreliably, through the arrack-addled mind of the dying narrator, and in truth we learn precious little about him. That said, he once had his own ESPNcricinfo profile, and a web page complete with grainy images dedicated to his achievements. Amongst these, he was the man behind pinch-hitting, advising Murali not to change his action, and encouraging the Sri Lankans to sledge. Volatile in character and dogged by bad luck and unsympathetic management, Pradeep is a character who really should have been real, his tale capturing the chaotic essence of Sri Lankan cricket brilliantly.

6) DAVID WISEMAN

Wondrous Oblivion (2003, dir. Paul Morrison)

The 11-year-old boy at the centre of this 2003 film is a poignant and recognisable figure to many sports fans: a cricket lover who's no good at cricket. Already something of an outsider growing up in Sixties London as the son of wartime Jewish immigrants, he is placed as scoreboard monitor rather than player. That is, until a cricket-mad Jamaican family move in next door and allow him to practise, become better, ever-more transfixed by the game, and, eventually, successful and popular. Wiseman is a young protagonist at the heart of a story about people on the fringes who fight for acceptance in an often-hostile environment.

5) DETECTIVE SERGEANT LEWIS

Inspector Morse: "Deceived by Flight" (1989, dir. Anthony Simmons)

Detective Chief Inspector Morse: everyone's favourite opera-loving, ale-slurping rozzer-romantic. Fond of the line "Fancy a pint, Lewis?" and perpetually in thrall to flame-haired sirens in beige culottes harbouring dark pasts, Morse bestrode our TV screens for years, solving highbrow murders with plucky Lewis, his Geordie serf, faithfully by his side. "Deceived by Flight" (geddit?) sees Lewis infiltrate an Oxford cricket team in an effort to uncover the true cause of the recent death of one of their players. The cricket scenes are as you'd expect. We get all the clichés – the dashing No.3, the boisterous grandee/umpire, the eager young 'un, the too-loud call of "RUN!" – and then Lewis himself, a rather canny leg-spin bowler who threatens to blow his cover by being a bit too good. Lewis emerges as perhaps the finest post-war leggie this country has produced.

4) BHUVAN
Lagaan (2001, Ashutosh Gowariker)

Bhuvan is the hero of the film (one of the greatest cricket movies going) in which a group of Indian villagers challenge the unfair British rulers' taxation by taking up cricket and challenging their imperial masters to a game. Bravery, leadership, love of cricket: the handsome Bhuvan is a fine protagonist.

3) JB
Million Dollar Arm (2014, dir. Craig Gillespie)

"How fast do they pitch in cricket?" As soon as you hear that, you know you're in trouble. Jon Hamm – he of the professional womanising in *Mad Men* – stars as sports agent JB Bernstein in this cricketing work. It's an attempt to retell the true story of Rinku Singh and Dinesh Patel, two young Indian lads who were taken over to trial for Major League Baseball franchises after winning a reality TV show. The reason the show exists, according to the film, is India's love of cricket and the therefore abundant number of cricketers ready to transfer their supposedly preternatural skills from the pitch to the diamond. The plan, much like the film, doesn't quite work, but it does show highlights of Andrew Strauss batting, so he's basically a Hollywood star.

2) HOOKER KNIGHT
Glory Gardens (1990s, Bob Cattell)

In a terrific series of cricket books for children (and a few grown-ups) following a young cricket team, there were many notable characters: Tylan Vellacott, the mercurial leg-spinner with a propensity to be expensive (unlike the socks he sold on his dad's market stall at weekends, severely impacting his availability for selection), or Jason Padgett, the promising youngster who gave up after two years to pursue his chess career. But it has to be the captain and co-founder of the side: Hooker Knight, a talismanic all-rounder who led a varied group of egos on almost implausibly regular and dramatic cup runs. A fine young man and a committed student of the game. No relation of Nick's.

1) FLASHMAN

Tom Brown's School Days (1857, Thomas Hughes); *Flashman* series (1977, George MacDonald Fraser)

One of life's unpleasant truths: being an awful person doesn't prevent you from being dynamite on the cricket pitch. Such is the case with Harry Paget Flashman, the swaggering bully of *Tom Brown's School Days* and the star of a series of novels by George MacDonald Fraser, in which he prowls the Victorian era like an unholy anti-Jonah, his every act of epic cowardice misconstrued as heroism. However, with ball in hand, Flash had the stuff. Invited to turn out for a Rugby Old Boys XI at Lord's, he records cricket's first-ever hat-trick and triumphs over an array of great (non-fictional) cricketers, including the fantastically named Fuller Pilch, a giant of the game years before the letters "WG" had ever been placed next to each other in a sentence. ∎

Iconic Fashion Statements

FROM LOVE BEADS TO OVERSIZED SPECS,
CRICKETERS HAVE ALWAYS EXPRESSED THEIR
SENSE OF "PERSONAL STYLE"

10) WAUGH'S COLLAR

A little detail that spoke volumes. Just as Eric Cantona starched his United collar so it would stand proud – he understood such things – so Mark Waugh, the most immaculate man in whites since Jeremy Irons punted down the River Cherwell, was a dedicated devotee of the upturned collar. With the look completed by the white sunhat, short-sleeved jumper and early-era shades, an enigmatic air followed Waugh around the cricket field. That majestic collar, with top button always done up, was the trademark touch.

9) SMITH'S NECKERCHIEF

Being a modest sort, Robin Smith probably only wore a neckerchief in India in 1993 because he was a bit hot. But for our purposes we've chosen to attach an imperialist symbolism to that rag around his neck, for it was none other than Douglas Jardine himself who first made the neckerchief popular, and of course, no English cricketer ever fought so hard to preserve the Empire. We'd like to think that the Judge, stylish and cool as ever, was merely carrying on the tradition.

8) RICHIE'S WRISTWATCH

When Richie Richardson batted in his watch, as he did most of the time, it wasn't because he was fussed about punctuality. The actual time – minutes, hours, all that – was not very important. "Tell me Viv," Richie never said, "how shall I proceed, given that my timepiece confirms there are 12 minutes until the luncheon interval? Perhaps caution may be the order of the day?" The simple truth was that Richie loved making mugs of fast bowlers, and so the watch was a prop, a snub to "nasties" everywhere – a clear message to any quicks out there that they'd never hit him. It elevated the nose-thumbing arrogance of the maroon sunhat to new degrees of cheek, and emasculated the world's slingers to clinic-dwelling impotents before they'd even bowled a ball.

7) SEHWAG'S BANDANA

Quite a few cricketers favour the bandana these days, lending as it does a certain defiant panache to the premature baldness issue afflicting virtually all of them. The bandana works as a halfway house between, say, Dave Houghton's proudly shiny pate and the re-thatched con trick of a startlingly hirsute Warne. It applies to the balding batsman a degree of street style that a lack of real hair has clearly deprived him of, without having to resort to the absurd "studio work" beloved of Warne, Gooch, Kallis, Narcissus et al. And Sehwag – beset up top by a surface of unsettling, isolated tufts – was the coolest bandana-wearer this side of Springsteen's guitarist.

6) BIG BENN'S FLARES

Flares, of course – from Lillee to Warne, via Big Bird Joel and "Nice Guy" Eddie Hemmings – have always been a part of cricket's DNA. But no modern player has pulled them off with such feverish glitterball-chutzpah as that great West Indian circus act, "Big"

Sulieman Benn. The Bajan spinner fancies himself rotten, bowls supremely tricky donkey-drops, and has been known to attend Chrissy Gayle's "party events". And in his quest to become the coolest sportsman in the world, he makes great use of his lengthy pins by sporting a pair of expertly-cut flares – stilts wrapped in pillowcases. And why? Because he can.

5) CLIVE'S NHS GLASSES

These were magisterial, steel-rimmed super-specs for the sort of man who values substance over fanciness; eye-shields for the man of action, hefty bins for the leader of consequence. No fripperies, no cutesy rimless fancies, and *definitely* no contact lenses (leave those for advertising execs and opening batsmen from Yorkshire), Clive Hubert Lloyd was a different beast altogether, the West Indian godfather, in touch with the higher consciousness and pioneering the heavy-duty NHS-style of bifocal a full three decades before posturing trustafarians with 20-20 vision decided they wanted to look like Mark Ronson. Clive would *not* be impressed.

4) WARNE'S BOWLING BOOTS

The Blond, staggering through customs with his charge sheet of naughtiness, badly out of form and nursing a dodgy shoulder, was dismissed as washed-up in 2005. But Warnie was channelling Vegas-era Elvis that summer, carrying off the mother of all comebacks to take 40 Ashes wickets, and doing it all in striking pairs of red-tinged tenpin-bowling boots and billowing strides. Even the wicket celebration – down on one knee, arms pumping, eyes bulging – had a touch of that "Suspicious Minds" encore about it. Only Warne could have got away with it.

3) SHARMA'S LOVE BEADS

The Westernisation of Indian culture has been well covered, and those shimmering über-cricketalists from the East went a step further by throwing the new ball to an extra from *Boogie Nights*. With a body-ratio of roughly 20 per cent flesh to 80 per cent jewellery, Ishant Sharma looks less like a manly fast bowler than he does a dazed, pubescent Woodstock victim.

2) GOWER'S BLUE SOCKS

"A patriotic gesture and a bit of fun" is David Gower's laconic take on his blue batting socks. Though the fun bit may have been lost on England's chairman of selectors Peter May, as well as the uniforms in charge – Squadron Captain Gooch and Major General Stewart – who grumbled on about a lack of seriousness in Gower's approach. To be fair, the logic was impenetrable. "How dare he make hundreds in blue socks when the rest of us are making fifties in grey ones? Take them off, man! Think of the team! Think of the grandchildren! Think of, think of, think of... England!"

1) VIV'S SWEATBANDS

Viv Richards never forgot where he came from or what he was here for. Back when the West Indies cricket team truly mattered to a region fighting for identity, Richards was a gleaming expression of what could be achieved when God-given ability met a mighty hard-ass. He was the boy from the Leewards who conquered the world, a whirlwind of runs, passion and pride, all encased in two sensationally brilliant Rasta sweatbands. Richards wasn't just belting bowlers through mid-wicket for his own sake, or even for the sake of his team; Viv was Viv, the King (after Marley) of the whole damn Caribbean, a shimmering man of the people, and their humble representative – and those bands on his wrists were there to prove it. ∎

Impersonations

AIN'T NOTHING LIKE THE REAL THING, SANG
MARVIN GAYE. TRY TELLING THIS LOT...

10) BALLS-UP AT THE BEEB

Former Pakistan wicketkeeper Nadeem Abbasi was understandably miffed when it emerged that an imposter had appeared on the BBC on numerous occasions pretending to be him. Nadeem Alam of Huddersfield had shared his views on Pakistani cricket on BBC World News, BBC Asian Network and Radio 5 Live despite his experience of the game amounting to a few games for his local club. Alam, who also admitted to posing as a squash player to blag free equipment, said: "I like to think I have been talking good cricket." Abbasi, who played three Tests in 1989, took it all in his stride, saying: "If I ever find Nadeem Alam, I will punch him in the face for damaging my country's reputation."

9) WILLIAM "MR GILBERT" GRACE

The 2005 Ashes has no shortage of oft-retold quirks and side-stories. But who remembers comedian Greg Davies' appearance as WG Grace in Channel 4's ads for the series that magical summer? Dressed in full Victorian cricketer garb – standing at 6ft 8in with fulsome beard and bulging belly to boot – Davies (who later became famous as Mr Gilbert in *The Inbetweeners*) spent the ads barking instructions and exhortations in the imagined mode of "The Doctor". He was even contracted by Channel 4 to make public appearances in the crowd at the five Tests – as well as other major sporting events like Wimbledon – boisterously shouting "Come on, England" at a variety of inopportune moments.

8) FIBBER IN THE HEAT

"Miles Jupp? Who the f***'s that?" So the *Rev* actor, Radio 4 *News Quiz* host and stand-up comedian was "welcomed" by one member of the established press pack during England's 2006 tour of India. Cricket-fanatic Jupp – having finished his starring role as Archie the Inventor in the stage version of *Balamory* and at that time still relatively unknown – had blagged his way onto the tour by bluffing the *Western Mail* and BBC Radio Scotland that he was a bona fide journalist, despite having no idea what he was doing. Jupp retold his experiences – he had little real work to do, but did spend time propping up the bar with David Gower – in a book and one-man show, *Fibber in the Heat*. Later – now very much a fan, having given up on the journo impression – he appeared on *Celebrity Mastermind* and chose "The life and career of Michael Atherton" as his specialist subject, eventually going on to win.

7) FRED SINGS THE KING

Having taken Elvis Presley to his heart as a youth working in a record shop, Andrew Flintoff's been an impersonator ever since, happy to offer a rendition whenever prompted. And he did just that in the winter of 2015 while playing for Brisbane Heat in the Big Bash League. Fielding at long-leg, Fred belted out "In The Ghetto" to millions of viewers over the player-mic in between balls.

6) COPYING HIS LONG RUN

Graham Gooch and Alastair Cook share it all – Essex, runs, batting, runs, Essex. They're simple men, they're exceptionally good players and they can both do a passable impression of Bob Willis bowling – Gooch on many an occasion, Cook in the summer of 2014 to take his sole Test wicket. It would be uncharitable to say it's their only form of expression but we have it on good authority that so impressed was Cook by Gooch's impression of Bob that he insisted on playing the curly-haired seamer in his Year 4 nativity, so he could "do the run-up". A long run, a fixed stare and a pumping right arm later, and Bethlehem didn't know what had hit it.

5) WHAT-CHU TALKIN' 'BOUT, WILLIS?

Joe Root took the mimicry of Bob Willis a step further after England sealed their 2015 Ashes win at Trent Bridge, donning a mask with a sizeable schnoz and sending up the former paceman in a dressing-room interview with Ian Ward. Consummate pro he may be, but even Ward couldn't keep a straight face as "Willis" gave England's bowlers 4/10 for yet another lacklustre display. The real Bob, surprisingly enough, was left unimpressed, noting that Root's impression was closer to Brian Clough.

4) THE SWANN AND ONLY

Graeme Swann is pretty good at impressions and he's done a lot of them. Being a less-than-sharp colleague of his can't always have been the most fun because you can be sure you'd have been the target of some joshing. His Kevin Pietersen, for example, is really very impressive – as evidenced in the summer of 2015 on *Willow Talk*, a show on the Australian radio station Triple M. He's variously tried his hand at grumpy Jimmy, little Rooteh, daft Bressy and Jonathan Trott – and they're all worth a listen. Destined for the world of entertainment, he was.

3) BREMNER TAKES A STAND

Satirist Rory Bremner has been sending up politicians and celebrities for years, most notably on Channel 4's hit comedy sketch show *Bremner, Bird and Fortune,* and cricket's never been far from his gaze. A fanatic of the game, Bremner's 1995 video release *Creased Up* saw him over-dubbing the voices of Gooch, Gower and Benaud to rib-tickling effect, and he was the natural choice to front the ECB's "Stand Up For T20" campaign in 2012, nailing Bumble and Boycott to a tee and helping flog some tickets in the process.

2) A REAL VAUGHAN IN THE SIDE

This was a lovely idea. Goldsborough second XI made headlines in 2006 after they were dismissed for 5: ten of their 11 batsmen went for ducks (their No.11 got a nice 0 not out). So, a year later, in stepped NatWest to reward their notoriety with something positive. Michael Vaughan was parachuted into the side for the game against Dishforth CC, disguised as "Gary Watson" – complete with prosthetics, a wig and padding. Gary, or the "long-haired lover from Liverpool" as one confused Goldsborough fan termed the mystery man, came in at 17 for 3 and was soon impressing everyone with his strokeplay. Unfortunately he nicked off for 28 and departed with the score on 48 for 5. Still, nice idea.

1) SILLY BILLY

Perhaps the most famous of the cricket impressionists, Billy Birmingham – aka The Twelfth Man – made quite a name for himself with his takes on the Channel 9 comms team, most notably as "Richie Benaud". He riffs, amongst other things, on the great man's love of beige or off-white jackets, his pronunciation of the word "two", the size of Bill Lawry's nose and the questionably fertile area of foreigners' names. ∎

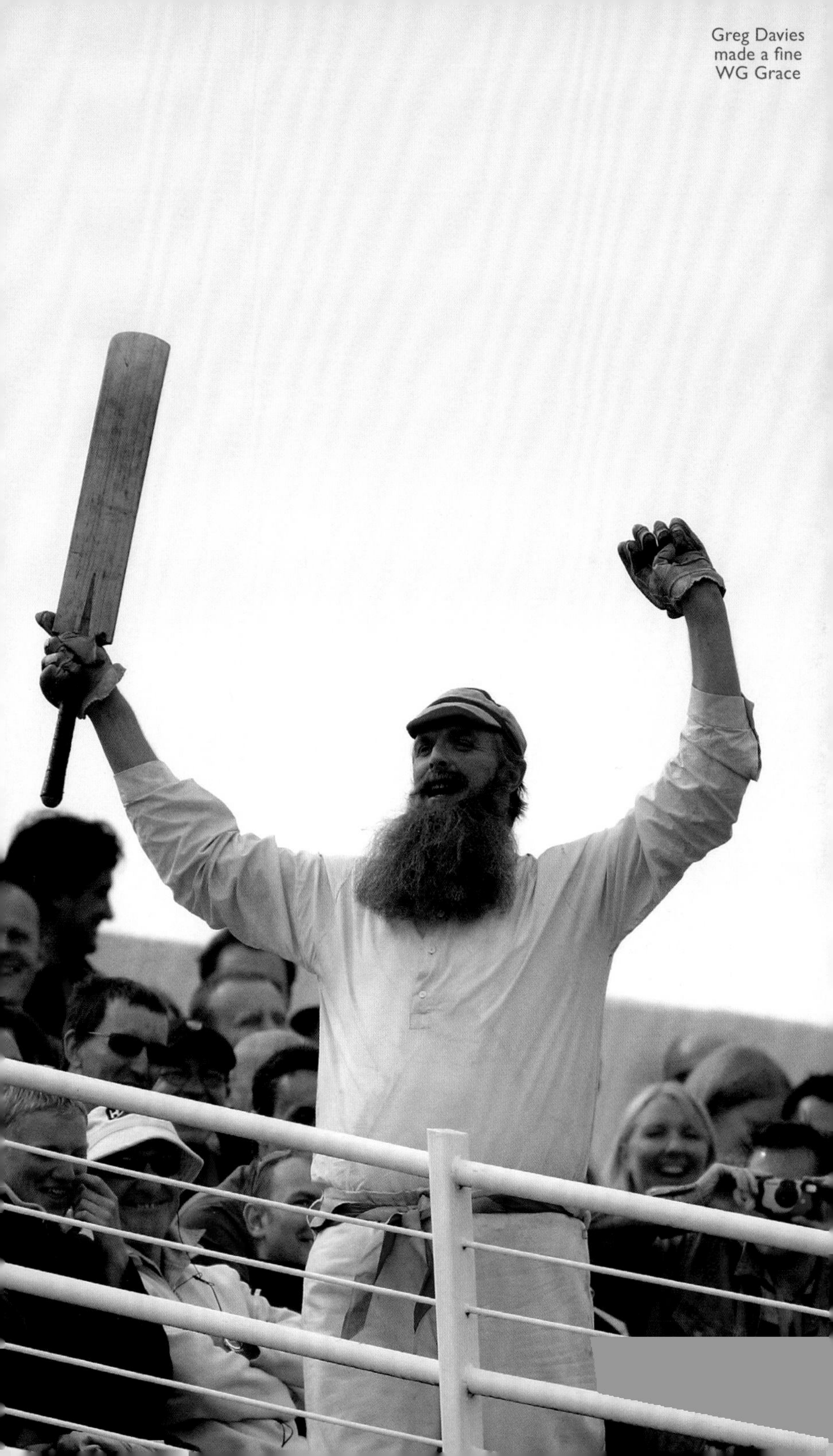

Greg Davies made a fine WG Grace

Bob Taylor needed some kit after making an unexpected return to Test cricket

Borrowed Kit

CRICKETERS TEND TO BE RATHER PARTICULAR ABOUT THEIR GEAR BUT SOMETIMES IT PAYS TO MIX THINGS UP A BIT

10) MALCOLM FINDS THE MIDDLE

Devon Malcolm scored just two half-centuries in his 304-game first-class career and in Test cricket he averaged only 6 with a highest score of 29. That score came at Sydney in 1995 and it came – drum roll, please – with a bat that didn't belong to him. There's every chance, knowing Dev's eyesight, that he'd picked up the wrong piece of willow but, whatever was behind it, it worked, as he smashed Shane Warne into the Sydney stands for a massive six.

9) THE WORM NOT RETURNED

Simon Jones' virtuoso display of reverse-swing in the 2005 Ashes has gone down in English cricket folklore but his batting cameos shouldn't be forgotten. Where would England have been without those frenzied last-wicket partnerships with Flintoff at Edgbaston and Hoggard at Trent Bridge? That glorious summer may have lost some of its sparkle. And who do we have to thank for Jones' batting efforts? Kevin Pietersen, of course. Not much fancying his Puma stick, Jones nabbed one of Kev's back-up Woodworm blades and swapped the stickers. The bat, described by Jones as "an absolute gun", helped him to a series average of 33 – more than double his career record.

8) NOTTS A LAUGHING MATTER

Jason Gallian was another who borrowed kit from Kevin Pietersen; only he didn't treat it quite as nicely. The Notts skipper, furious after Pietersen told him he was unhappy at the club and would be seeking a move, signed off the 2003 county season by reportedly hurling KP's bag from the Trent Bridge balcony and breaking his bat. "I got a call saying the captain had trashed my equipment," he recalled. Pietersen threatened to take Notts to a tribunal to force through his exit but eventually saw out the final year of his contract before moving to Hampshire. Everyone lived happily ever after. Sort of.

7) SHIK'S NEW STICK

Having waited nine seasons for his first crack at Test cricket, Shikhar Dhawan's chance finally came at Mohali in 2013 in place of his mentor Virender Sehwag. Oddly, the Indian left-hander decided this was a good opportunity to try a new bat, having picked up one of Murali Vijay's in the nets and liked the feel of it. A few days later he and Vijay walked out to the middle to face Australia and shared an opening stand of 289, Dhawan blitzing his way to the fastest Test century by a debutant. Using the same borrowed stick, he went on to finish as top run-scorer at the 2013 ICC Champions Trophy.

6) RUNNING THE GAUNTLETS

Stand-in wicketkeepers are always fun. Anthony McGrath did it at Lord's in 2003, Vikram Solanki tried it out at the World T20 in

2007, and even Paul Collingwood had a go, at Chester-le-Street in 2009. But they were still professional cricketers – not yet retired, and not yet two glasses into their day in the corporates. Bob Taylor, as skilled as he may have been, must have been surprised to get the call during England's Test match against New Zealand in 1986. Bruce French was concussed so Taylor, 45 years of age and entertaining guests for Cornhill, was called for. He borrowed French's whites, nabbed his keeping gear from temporary stand-in Bill Athey, kept for the rest of the day and went on to meet the Queen.

5) SHIRT OFF HIS BACK

Dave Whelan (not the bloke who used to be Wigan FC's chairman) probably never expected to be asked to lend his England shirt to Paul Collingwood. The England fan, watching his side in Antigua in 2014, learned that his new red ODI replica shirt was needed by England's fielding coach Collingwood when the Durham man was pressed into stepping in as an auxiliary substitute fielder. Whelan duly obliged and his shirt – a Christmas present bought by his wife and only being worn for the first time – made its way to the England changing-room.

4) BIFF'S BURGERS

Arriving at the SCG for the final day of South Africa's third Test against Australia in 2009, Graeme Smith would not have wanted to bat. His side were one wicket down, needing to avoid being bowled out to save the game, and Biff was in the wars. He had a broken hand and a sore elbow that had required injections, but with 8.2 overs to go, he strode out. Problem was, he hadn't bothered bringing his kit. With no alternative, he had to borrow Jacques Kallis' shirt and Paul Harris' burger sauce-stained jumper. Battered and bruised, Smith eventually fell to Johnson after a courageous 30 minutes at the crease, but what a triumph of determination that natty old sweater played host to.

3) RAMPS IS A NEW MAN

Mark Ramprakash was a well-known bat-obsessive, meticulous to the last in ensuring that everything was exactly as it should be with his blade. So when he broke his beloved Gray-Nicolls shortly after hitting his 99th first-class century in 2008, a deathly hush enveloped the Surrey dressing-room. The tension mounted as ten innings went by without so much as a fifty, Ramps trying out five new bats before discarding each of them. It was only after borrowing a Gray-Nicolls from his practice partner Scott Newman that he was able to break the hoodoo, hitting a ton at Headingley to become the 25th batsman – and very possibly the last – to score 100 first-class hundreds.

2) AN ABSOLUTE STEELE

The year 1975 was a golden one for David Steele – and it's a year that demonstrates the importance of not having to borrow. The silver fox was in good form before his county Northants faced up against Sussex, captained by then-England skipper Tony Greig. Unfortunately for Steele, his kit – including his new Duncan Fearnley bat – had been half-inched. He had to borrow replacement kit, and his form duly dropped; he would only score 7 and 8 against Greig's Sussex. But then, a week before his Test debut at Lord's, salvation: the thief called up, wracked with guilt, and offered to return his kit. The bank clerk had his weapon back.

1) PRIME BEEF

Ian Botham was so good that he couldn't care less whose kit he got his sweaty macho hands on. In 1981 at Leeds he bludgeoned the Aussies using Gooch's Duncan Fearnley, reasoning that "Goochie hadn't used it much in the match and I thought there were a few runs left in it." A few years later at Worcestershire, he nabbed one of Graeme Hick's cherished Fearnley 405s, got runs and ended up using it for the season; and he was so good that sometimes he didn't bother using anything at all. During a tour game for England in Australia in which he turned up catastrophically the worse for wear, he stumbled out of the gate and got halfway to the crease with England two wickets down, before a fieldsman pointed out that taking guard might prove tricky without a bat. With our hero still reeking of last night, England's twelfth man ran the blade out to him, ushering Sir Ian to the middle, where inevitably, and exceedingly Beefily, he smashed a brilliant 70. ∎

Naughty rascal Karl
Power walked out to
bat for England during
the 2001 Ashes

Hoaxes and Imposters

NOTABLE CASES OF SUBTERFUGE AND SILLINESS

10) MAJOR COUP

Immediately after World War II, Surrey needed to appoint a new captain and chose Major Leo Bennett, a successful club cricketer from the local area. Soon after the decision was made, a fellow Bennett, Major Nigel Harvie, came down to The Oval to renew his membership. So the story goes, the club chairman presumed this Bennett was the other, and the wrong man was offered the job. But far from correcting the error, Major Nigel happily took the reins. A batting average of 16 and Surrey's worst County Championship finish of 11th saw *Wisden* record that "want of knowledge on the field presented an unconquerable hindrance to the satisfactory accomplishment of the Major's arduous duties... which prejudiced the general work of the side". Bennett was relieved of his "arduous duties" at the end of the 1946 season, his audacious mark in history made.

9) ADRIAN SHAM-KAR

County blagger Adrian Shankar rewrote his CV to create a fictitious alter ego: one who was younger, and better at cricket.

Lancashire and Worcestershire were both duped by his birth-date and run-scoring claims before he and his fake documentation were rumbled in 2011 two weeks into a two-year deal at New Road. He turned out to be three years older than he had stated and his claims about first-class run-scoring in Sri Lanka were proved pure hokum. (He hadn't played football for Arsenal's academy or national-level tennis, either.) He'd actually averaged 19 in just a handful of first-class games before finally being outed and sacked.

8) POWER TO THE PEOPLE

During the fourth Ashes Test in 2001, renowned prankster Karl Power (he of Manchester United's Champions League photo-bomb) strolled to the wicket, confusing fans and players alike. Power was hiding in the changing-room before the game. One of his friends was meant to call him at the fall of a wicket and then Power would stride to the crease, hopefully to face Shane Warne. Unfortunately for him, he got a different call, and went out onto the pitch anyway, in full batting gear, even though Nasser Hussain was already in the middle. He got another call, lifted his helmet, and walked off again to applause from an amused crowd.

7) A "SPOT" OF BOTHER

Mazher Mahmood – the infamous "Fake Sheikh" of the erstwhile *News of the World* – was the undercover journalist to expose Salman Butt, Mohammad Asif and Mohammad Amir in the spot-fixing scandal of 2010. Mahmood, posing as an Indian businessman interested in setting up a cricket tournament for betting purposes, secretly filmed conversations with the players' agents in a London hotel. After the trio were caught out, and subsequently banned, they told the court that they'd had reservations as to the legitimacy of the Sheikh. Should've trusted that gut feeling, boys. In 2016 Mahmood ran into some trouble with the law himself as he was found guilty of tampering with trial evidence.

6) IPL "INSIDER"

In the second IPL season in 2009, an anonymous blog about the Kolkata Knight Riders – called Fake IPL Player – hit the headlines for its criticism of teammates, coaches and even the franchise owners. On its busiest day, the controversial site – which was believed to be the work of a disgruntled fringe player – gained over 150,000 visitors and is estimated to have received around 37,000 hours of exposure, as well as causing a cross-platform media frenzy in India. A year later though, unheard-of Bangalorean marketing specialist Anupam Mukerji revealed himself as the blog's true author, admitting that he had "never met a cricketer in my life".

5) HOSPITAL PASS

With coach Bob Simpson in hospital after an operation on the 1995 West Indies tour, Australian opener Michael Slater thought he would get into the heavily sedated coach's good books by visiting him in hospital. But Simpson, sluggish of mind due to the medication, mistook Slater for his teammate Justin Langer. Slater encouraged Langer to visit, thinking that he'd now get the credit he deserved. But Simpson, who grew more compos mentis every day, simply thanked Langer for a second trip that went way beyond the call of duty. Come The Oval in 2001, Langer would happily nick Slater's spot at the top of the Aussie order, too.

4) SELECTION BURN

Team selection has never been easy. Ahead of Australia's 1890 tour of England, the selectors chose the Tasmanian Ken Burn as back-up wicketkeeper to the legendary Jack Blackham. A letter was dispatched inviting Burn to join the touring party. It was only after the group had set sail from Adelaide that a fairly substantial blunder was uncovered: this supposed reserve stumper – though a competent batsman and occasional seamer – had never donned the gauntlets in anger. Somewhere, along the creaking lines of 19th-century communication, someone had got the wrong Burn. Ken's performances were perfectly respectable, but poor old Blackham was without cover behind the sticks for the whole trip.

3) ON THE HUNT FOR RL HUNTE

Errol Hunte, West Indian wicketkeeper of the 1930s, played three Tests. But when you scurry off to check that fact in a contemporary edition of *Wisden,* it will appear that he only played two. So what's the explanation? Well, it's actually the *Almanack* that has the matter wrong. During one of Errol's three games a mistaken scorer wrote his first name as the initials "RL" in the book. It took a full 40 years for the mistake to be rectified, and the fictional one-Test wonder – the imposter RL Hunte – was deprived of his first and only Test cap. It was reassigned to Errol, who was rightly awarded his third.

2) THE UNFORTUNATE MR SMITH

In 1933 the Essex leg-spinner Peter Smith was in a Chelmsford cinema when a message flashed up on the screen telling him to report to his county immediately. His excited father then produced a telegram from the Essex secretary, who later confirmed the news on the phone: Smith had been chosen for the next day's Test. He dashed to The Oval on an early train the next morning. Having made his way to the changing-room, Smith asked the captain if he had made the final XI. Bob Wyatt, standing in as skipper for the injured Douglas Jardine, told Smith he had no knowledge of his selection in the first place. The telegram had been a fake. "The poor fellow," Wyatt later wrote. "He had been made the victim of a cruel hoax."

1) THE CLUB THAT WASN'T THERE

The hoax to beat all others. Post-war ad-man Les Williamson, a north Londoner with a vivid imagination – and a small group of his pals – invented an entire cricket club: the St Pancras Spartans. Every week of the 1951 and '52 seasons, the eccentric tricksters sent in detailed, fictitious match reports that were devotedly published in the local paper. As well as tall tales of on-field goings-on, there were news stories, like the retirement of the club's long-serving groundsman who, in a "happy ceremony", was presented with a miniature silver lawnmower and roller. ∎

Are the days of the fourth umpire numbered?

Jobs for the Boys (and Girls)

THE PLUMBEST, TOUGHEST AND ODDEST GIGS IN THE GAME

10) PLAYER/COMMENTATOR

Not to be confused with the player (generally old school) who joins the boys in the box when he's not required out in the middle, only to be told – within minutes – they'd "best get the pads on" following an inevitable flurry of wickets. We're talking about the young lad (with aspirations) at deep square leg "on the mic", the one who's about to be screamed at by his captain because instead of coming up to save the single he's chatting to Paul Allott about Adele and pizza. Still, it's a foot in the door, eh?

9) CHARACTER SCORER

As a character-doyen of the scoring fraternity, the late Bill Frindall – much-loved Bearded Wonder and *Test Match Special* immortal – was something of a lone cuckoo. But these days, in Sky TV world, the scorer as "a bit of a character" is an absolute prerequisite of the gig. And so we have the peculiar spectacle of Benedict Bermange, Sky's main scorer and a gentle, decent fellow who's good with numbers, being ribbed and poked by Sir Ian and the rest (well, mainly Sir Ian) as if he's some kind of dots-joining medieval bear summoned from market to dance for the barons.

8) FOURTH UMPIRE

Just as the farmhand joins the dole queue next to the nobbled old grocer, so the fourth umpire shivers at the back behind the miller on Jobseeker's, sadly thumbing his P45. Why? Because progress waits for no man. For years the reserve-reserve umpire had been a ghostly yet permanent fixture at international matches; waiting for a sign, lurking in his blacked-out hovel and emerging only to watch the groundsman rolling the pitch at lunch or when summoned by his bronzed on-field superiors for "a change of ball". But following the news that a different ball was to be used at each end of an ODI innings, the fourth umpire found himself robbed of that critical moment when he gets to bring the box of balls out at 34 overs. Not all jobs in cricket's marketplace are assured; in these straitened times his days are surely numbered.

7) DESIGNATED PRANKSTER

All teams naturally contain a good mix of characters, and everyone's got their own gag-meister who can balance a mug of wee on the top of a door. But while letting a rat loose in the team bath or smothering the captain's genitals in peat displays a psychological nuance in its protagonist that should be valued, it's a bad sign when a gentleman's dressing-room capabilities are cited as a key reason for his presence in the team at all. Runs, wickets, catches? Nah, but he's a genius with a ferret.

6) BUZZ CREATOR

You're tired. You're not playing that great. Your keeping's alright – not that anyone notices – but you can't buy a run. The baby's been up all night – tonsillitis. The wife's not been sleeping. You're 230 behind on first innings and you've got to bat last. The sun's out: a batting day. The skipper leads out, stern, collar up, pensive; and right behind him is you, the designated buzz creator, the craftsman of chirp. Your stature (5ft 7in, 5ft 8in at a push) and breeding (lower-middle-class; wicketkeeper) ensures that you must remain optimistic at all times. You are smiley, excitable and ready with your soaring phrases and punchy buzzwords. "Our day today, fellas!" You're a natural extrovert. "One brings two, lads!" It's the end of another wicket-less over. You'll clap your mittened hands together – a sad, dull thud – and start your jaunty jog up to the other end. And you'll rifle through your repertoire one more time. And you'll think about the wife. And you'll pray she got some kip.

5) BALL SHINER

Balls have been shined for centuries. Once upon a time it was considered a job for all. Madness. These days, every self-respecting team in the land from under-nines upwards must contain one out-and-out specialist in the art of rubbing a cherry down the left flank of one's crotch. Alastair Cook is a case in point. Drier than a Jack Dee gag in the Atacama, Cook has an enviously underdeveloped sweat gland, meaning that he is able to keep the thing bone-dry on one side; moist, heavy and shiny on the other. This trait assigns him an almost unbearable mystery: how, if the human body is made up of 75 per cent water, does he manage to shed not a drop?

4) CHIEF WAG

Nothing is left to chance with Team England today. That's why Chantal Bell, ex-npower girl and now wife of Ian Ronald, became the officially appointed WAG Social Secretary, as confirmed by no less a personage than Mr Jonathan Agnew on *Test Match Special* during the 2011 Oval Test. With Bell having seemingly played his last for England, the post is now up for grabs.

3) MEDIA FRONTMAN

If you're any good, this is the plumbest and most lucrative job of all. Either your team's won and you're at the front of the queue, cheekily catching the mood and allowed to get away with the odd line the bosses might not approve of, or your team's lost and you're up there as the maverick free-thinker with a mandate to puncture the gloom by telling it like it is, cutting through the spin to say what all fans want to hear at that point. Which is basically: "Yep, we were crap. Sorry, folks."

2) TEAM SONG LEADER

It's a scientific fact that men who enjoy testosterone-filled dressing-rooms desire to sing team songs. But it's dangerous. Any abuse of "the song" can lead not just to violent outpourings of man-grief but to the very real collapse of the whole brothers-in-arms, back-to-back air-guitar model of existential blokeness – which buggers everything up. Recent studies revealing a correlation between Male Bicep Width (MBW) and Team Song Enthusiasm (TSE) suggests that some men value the singing of songs more than others. But thankfully this post-feminist watershed has yet to afflict the soldiers of Australia, whose in-house victory sacrament "Under The Southern Cross I Stand" is the dreary New Year's Eve party of team songs, made all the more mawkish and grave by its strained demands on togetherness. It makes for a tetchy affair: after a Test win in 2009 against India, Michael Clarke, whose turn it was to lead the chorus, tried to duck out because he had a date to keep with his girl. To a collapsing backdrop of horrified gasps and the swift fanning of flushed cheeks, Simon Katich choked back the tears to line the spirits of his forefathers across Clarke's path, pinning the human tattoo up against the wall until he honoured his duties. Now *that's* the smell of team spirit.

1) VILLAGE FATES

Job creation is not just confined to the pro game. Amateur teams are overflowing with titles, roles, responsibilities and tasks, with a strict feudal system in place to guard against anarchy. The end of a home game goes roughly like this: the kid collects the subs because (a) it's the worst job, and (b) it trains him/her for a future reliant on handouts; the teenagers move the sightscreens and pick up the boundary markers because they can smoke, drink and take their time in the doing of it; the fathers and club committee members lock up/dismantle the temporary nets and "rope off the square" because these are subtle sciences beyond the scope of today's youth; and finally, the fabled guardsman of the "Valees Bag" – that velvet-plastic Pandora's box of watches, wallets, heirlooms, war medals etc – is the sole job of the irreproachable senior pro. Without all this, club cricket would have died centuries ago. ∎

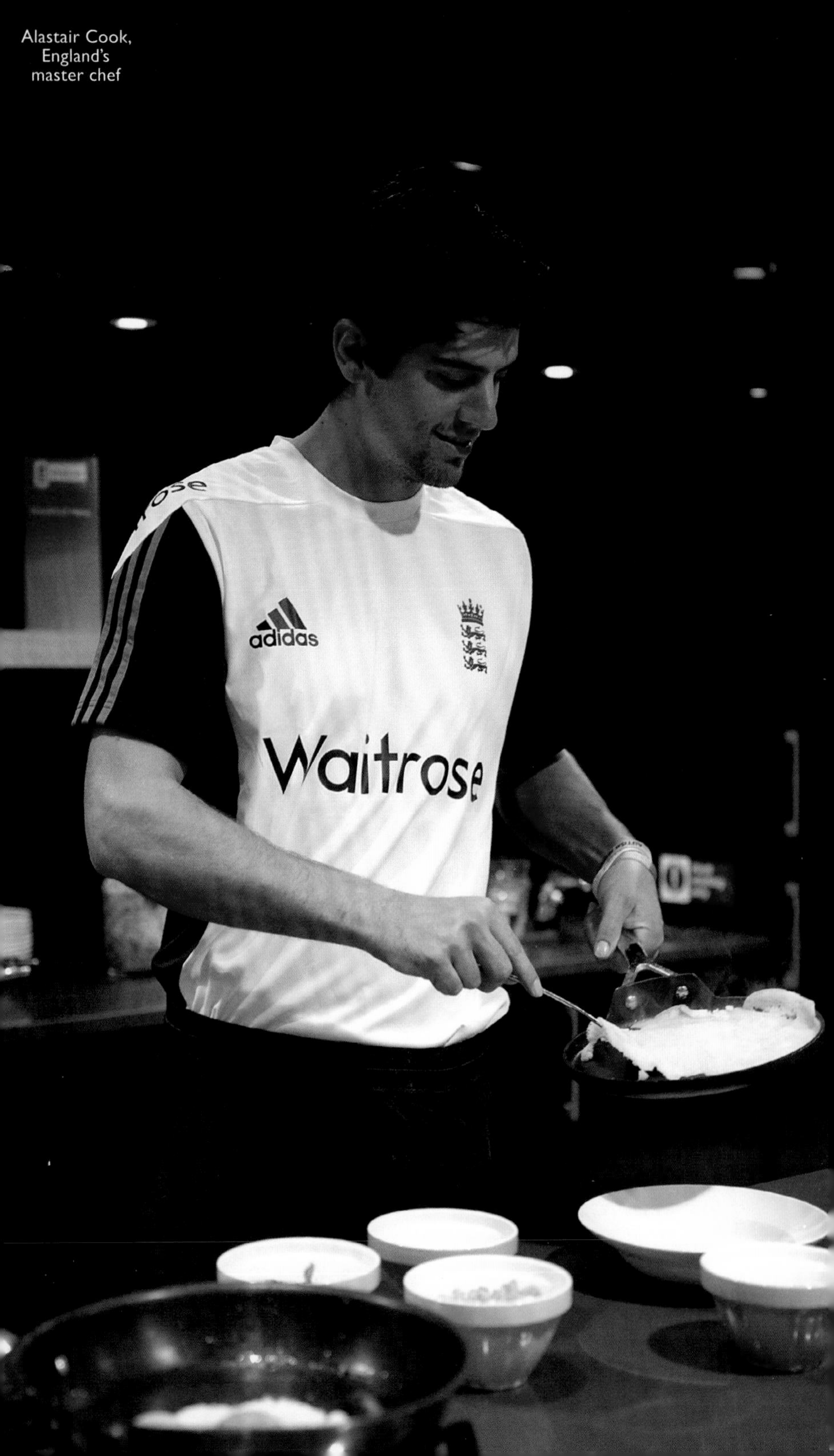

Alastair Cook,
England's
master chef

Cheese!

CRICKET IS GREAT. CHEESE MAKES IT BETTER.
READ ON CAERPHILLY...

10) BRIE TO CHEDDAR

There's only one place to start: "The Big Cheese", "Le Grand Fromage", "the Dairylea triangle thinking he's brie". Kevin Pietersen's descriptions of Matt Prior in his 2014 autobiography are numerous and cheesy. If Jarlsberg made wicketkeepers...

9) YOU'VE GOT TO FIGHT FOR THE RIGHT DOLCELATTE

Back in 1992, former Middlesex man Simon Hughes was having a nice bit of tucker with teammate Ian Botham. After a few wines – Botham's not averse to the odd sip of claret, you know – he fancied a bit of cheese, as all right-thinking people would.

"Can you bring me some Dolcetti?" he asked the waiter.

"Don't you mean Dolcelatte?" Hughes nipped in.

"That's what I said. Dolcetti," replied Botham.

"No, it's Dolcelatte," Hughes insisted.

Botham, by this stage suitably hacked off, retorted with the now infamous line: "Well, how many bloody Test wickets did you get?"

8) AUSSIES CHEESED OFF

At Trent Bridge, in the first Test of the 2013 Ashes series, Stuart Broad nicked a ball from Ashton Agar to slip, via Brad Haddin's glove, and didn't move. Much to everyone's surprise, including Broad's, he wasn't given out and went on to add 28 to his tally as England won the match by 14 runs. When Darren Lehmann accused Broad of "blatant cheating", the England seamer replied: "Cricket is quite an old-fashioned sport and is still viewed in some quarters as 'you should have a cup of tea and everything will be fine'. But let's make no mistake about it, we are not playing for a cheese sandwich, we are playing for an Ashes series." Later that year, in Australia, Broad and his mates won exactly as many Tests as a cheese sandwich would have.

7) A DIET FIT FOR A KING

Want to know what it takes to be one of the best cricketers of all time? Just follow the athletic diet plan of a certain Shane Warne. Back in 2005, when asked about his success and how his life had changed as a professional cricketer over the years, Warne said: "My diet is still pizzas, chips, toasted cheese sandwiches and milkshakes." He gets variation points for toasting his cheese but if he ditched the pizzas, chips and milkshakes in favour of a bit more cheese, he may have become one of the world's best.

6) BABYBEL STOPS PLAY

During Sri Lanka's 2014 tour of England, Shaminda Eranga managed to bag a bizarre double. Not only was he the victim of the least-celebrated hat-trick of all time (nobody – including the bowler, Stuart Broad – realising it had been taken), he was also struck by an ellipsoid-shaped cheese in the form of a Babybel (other cheeses are available). With the seamer minding his own business on the boundary at Headingley, the pasteurised projectile came from the Western Terrace stand behind him. Play was stopped as the umpires inspected the offending missile but Eranga got no sympathy from his teammates. "It was cheese, not a rock," explained a smiling Dinesh Chandimal, a man who has clearly never been struck by be-waxed Edam.

5) YES, CHEF

"Predictable, one-paced and not in keeping with modern culinary methods," imaginary critics may have said of Alastair Cook's decision to bake a cheese-and-onion tart for a charity cook-off if they were trying to make a lazy comparison with Cook's ODI record. Run by cricket charity Chance to Shine, the 2014 edition of Chance to Dine was the third such event and it was the third to be won by Alastair "Chef" Cook. "I genuinely can't believe that I've somehow managed to win with a cheese-and-onion tart," added England's Test skipper.

4) LAKER'S CHOICE

In the summer of 1956, Jim Laker, one of England's greatest ever bowlers, pulled off the incredible feat of taking 19 wickets in a Test match – you all know the story. But what you may not know is that the Surrey spinner chose to celebrate the record on his own with a pint and a cheese sandwich in his local pub.

3) BALL OF THE CENTURY

Close your eyes and you can still see it. Everyone's favourite cheese-eating leg-spinner rolls up to the crease and sends down that extraordinary delivery. Poor Mike Gatting at the other end can do nothing but helplessly watch it grip and turn past his bat. The moment is Warne's; Gatting is blameless to everyone. Well, not quite everyone: Graham Gooch, ever the joker, commented: "If it had been a cheese roll, it would never have got past him." It's a crazy comment, really. Hitting a cheese roll would be nigh on impossible due to its lack of bounce and the fact it has no ball-like features at all but, hey, maybe we're overanalysing it.

2) DINNER AT BOYCOTT'S

The idea of dinner at Geoff Boycott's doesn't immediately fill you with images of warm hearths and sing-alongs around the piano. In his autobiography (imaginatively titled *My Autobiography*) Dickie Bird recalls the one and only time he was invited over to lunch. "When I arrived at fortress Boycott, I found that the gates were locked, and Boycott, teasing me on the intercom, would not let me in." Classic. Bird then proceeded to climb over the wall and was met at the door by a smiling Boycs who invited him in for lunch. Unfortunately for Dickie, it wasn't everything he was hoping for: "I was looking forward to some Yorkshire puddings and roast beef, what I got was a toasted cheese sandwich."

1) BRESNAN BRINGS THE BRANSTON

England's Tim Bresnan enjoyed a year to remember in 2012. He continued his winning run in the national side (taking his tally of Test victories to a perfect 10 out of 10), signed his first central contract and played his part in England becoming the No.1 Test team in the world. Perhaps most importantly – individually at least – he was named one of *Wisden*'s Cricketers of the Year and was described, beautifully, by Tanya Aldred as having "the air of a man with an emergency cheese sandwich in his back pocket". When asked in a follow-up interview whether he had a cheese sandwich on him, Bresnan replied: "Yes. Yes, I do. It's got Branston Pickle on it as well." Saucy. ∎

Nicknames

10) MONDE "ALL HANDS" ZONDEKI

How much Monde Zondeki's teammates actually used this nickname is a moot point, but for its sheer ingenuity it makes our list. Thought up by English hacks during South Africa's tour of England in 2003, they were no doubt delighted when the leg-spinner-turned-paceman who liked to hit the "deck" hard was "handed" his Test debut at Headingley. Things didn't go too well with the ball, a side strain restricting him to 4.5 overs, but he hit a half-century from No.10 – his only fifty in first-class cricket – to help the Proteas to a big win. He played just five more Tests before retiring in May 2013 due to persistent injuries.

9) MIKE "FEC" ATHERTON

Short, unforgettable and really quite nasty, the "FEC" sobriquet was daubed on the young Michael's locker by one of Lancashire's furry beasts within weeks of the boy's emergence – via Manchester Grammar and Cambridge – into Old Trafford's macho, beery dressing-room. "Anybody with a further education was sneered at," Atherton later wrote of those early days in the Eighties, adding that while the initials were "assumed to stand for Future England Captain", in actual fact the middle word was "Educated" and the others, well, you can work out for yourself. "It was clear I was going to have to work hard to earn my stripes at Old Trafford," he added, "so I played down my Cambridge education as much as I could."

8) KEVIN "FIGJAM" PIETERSEN

He's been called a few other things in his time, both on and off the airwaves and in and out of earshot, but the most evocative and enduring of Kevin Pietersen's many monikers is Australia's effort from the 2006/07 Ashes tour, when the hosts abbreviated "F** I'm Good, Just Ask Me" to the cheeky and catchy "FIGJAM".

7) ASHLEY "KING OF SPAIN" GILES

With Gilo celebrating his benefit year in 2004 having belatedly been accepted as an England spin bowler, a load of merch emblazoned with the legend "The King of Spin" was ordered to prove it. But when a print error led to a batch of mugs coming back with "Spain" in place of "Spin", the old "Wheelie Bin" jibes, with their hints of haplessness, came flooding back. However, Giles rather brilliantly embraced it, turning a messy episode into an enduring nickname. The only person evidently unamused was a certain Juan Carlos of Madrid: "I do not know who this Ashley Giles is," the monarch announced, "but I can assure him that I am the King of Spain."

6) BERT "DAINTY" IRONMONGER

Born out of rural hardship in Australia in the 1880s, Bert was tough as old boots and anything but dainty – hence the contrary nickname. As a boy, he lost half his forefinger in a chaff-cutter and went on to work as a labourer on the railways before a late crack at professional cricket. He made his Sheffield Shield debut at the age of 33 and his Test debut 14 years after that, spinning the ball off the stump of his finger to great effect, taking 74 wickets in 14 Tests.